T0294887

OBLIVION OR UTOPIA

The Prospects for Africa

Chiku Malunga

Foreword by Alan Fowler

University Press of America,® Inc.
Lanham · Boulder · New York · Toronto · Plymouth, UK

Copyright © 2010 by
University Press of America,® Inc.
4501 Forbes Boulevard
Suite 200
Lanham, Maryland 20706
UPA Acquisitions Department (301) 459-3366

Estover Road
Plymouth PL6 7PY
United Kingdom

Library of Congress Control Number: 2009938778
ISBN: 978-0-7618-4985-8 (clothbound : alk. paper)
ISBN: 978-0-7618-4986-5 (paperback : alk. paper)
eISBN: 978-0-7618-4987-2

I dedicate this book to President Barack Obama for demonstrating to the whole world that nothing is impossible to those that believe.

Contents

Foreword

Much has been written about Africa's 'predicament'. This condition can be summarized as continued 'under-development' despite, or because of, trillions of dollars in aid. The investment has been accompanied by special UN programmes, as a priority for NGO-isms and a star-studded history of 'coalition for Africa style' impulses by Western political leaders and celebrities. For this author, similar initiatives and claims, for example, of the success of debt reduction, are a saddening celebration of the indignity of seemingly intractable economic dependency. Aided development, trading and commercial finance have still to remedy an immoral paradox where a bounty of the continent's natural resources actually sustain the deprivation of so many Africans whose rights are typically honoured in the breach. Yet, despite their plethora, the texts on the problems and potentials of Africa's development show Western biases and glaring gaps. This publication fills one area of neglect by looking and writing through a lens and towards an audience of young, privileged, African adults.

The book's central argument for economic independence founded on local value-added production using indigenous resources is familiar. However, novelty and value stem from an extraordinarily comprehensive exploration of impediments to reaching this objective. After dealing briefly with the usual suspects - poor leadership, corrupted governance, stifling of dissent, tolerance of mediocrity, unfair foreign subsidies, adverse trading conditions and so on - the text takes the reader on a journey less traveled in critical analysis. Amongst many others, explorations are to be found in discussion about the paucity of imagination on the continent that is not a mimic of elsewhere. There is an investigation of the what, where, why and how of political engagement by young people. Up for debate is the role of faith and how tensions between secular government and religious politics could be reconciled. Attention is focussed on why culture is so fundamental to Africa's development processes and so poorly understood. What can be done about endemic economic mind sets that buy foreign rather than African, that lack financial patriotism and show tendencies to waste rather than save? Looking further a field, what can(not) be learned from Asian experiences, such as South Korea, about a carefully proportioned, effective economic role for government. These are but some of the topics that weave a coherent and cogent tapestry.

The grounding and breadth of analysis is matched by an imagination-inspired set of detailed proposals that would re-position Africa not just towards the rest of the world but, more essentially, towards the economic independence required for self-definition. Some suggestions are aspirations, others are simply practical. Both are required. And, unlike many other proposals towards resolving the continents problems, there is a refreshing focus on the energies, roles and contributions of Africa's young people as generators, carriers and protagonists of a well-crafted endogenous agenda for development with dignity.

In short this is not 'just another book' about Africa's development. It is an unusual and uncompromising blend of emotion, reason, curiosity, knowledge and reflections on personal experience. If this is but one example of what Africa's younger generation is capable of conceiving and doing, utopia will eventually triumph over oblivion.

Professor Alan Fowler
Herbertsdale, South Africa

Acknowledgements

I owe my thanks to many people and organizations whose support made the writing of this book possible. I want to thank the leaders of the organizations I interviewed for the research. I want to thank all individuals I have been having discussions with over the years on the topic discussed in the book. I also want to thank all the organizations I have worked with in the capacity of a consultant or advisor in Africa, Europe and America. These have been my real classroom where I have learnt development practice as it really works on the ground.

Special thanks must go to the *'group of privileged professional young African adults'* who met in Antananarivo, Madagascar on 26th and 27th August 2008 to discuss the 'prospects for Africa'. My participation in that discussion resurrected this project which was by that time in a 'coma'.

I want to thank my three mentors Professor Alan Fowler, Professor Gomo Michongwe and Dr Rick James for helping me discover my voice and my place as an author. It was these three wonderful gentlemen who helped set me on the journey of self-discovery which led me to striving, often very painfully, with understanding the real nature and essence of the 'African problem'. They may not completely agree with where the journey has taken me to so far as reflected in the content of this book but that is what real mentorship is all about – helping those one is mentoring discover who they truly are and giving them the freedom to become who they are meant to be.

I want to recognize the Spirit. Thanks for occasionally waking me up in the middle of the night with insights in the form of the *still small voice* to give the content of the book a freshness that would not be possible otherwise.

I want to sincerely thank my wife, Chawanangwa, for always reminding me not to forget to take a notebook and a pen to put on the side of the pillow when going to sleep at night so that, 'when the Spirit comes in the cool and quiet of the night with insights in the form of the *still small voice* I can jot them down immediately before they fly away at dawn'. I want to thank her for bearing with me for frequently rising up from bed, sometimes numerous times in a night, to jot down the insights.

CHAPTER 1: INTRODUCTION

On 26th and 27th August, 2008, a group of young African professionals met at Hotel Panorama in Antananarivo, Madagascar, to discuss the future of Africa. The group sought to identify and explore the topmost African problem. The problem was identified as Africa's failure to transform its resources into wealth. Then ways and means to address this fundamental problem were explored. This was done through reflecting on the following strategic questions:

- What is development and what would a 'developed' Africa look like?
- Why have past and current efforts to develop Africa failed?
- What should Africa's topmost economic development priority be?
- Who should lead Africa's effort to economically catch up with the rest of the world?
- How can Africa break the aid dependence?
- Which other countries or regions have developed in the recent past?
- How did they do it? What can we learn from them?

A summary of the discussion is given in appendix one. The conclusion of the discussion was that Africa faces a bleak future unless it finds an alternative to the aid based development that has not really worked in the last fifty years. It was this discussion that played an inspiration in me to write this book. The discussion provided a framework that needed more content and meaning hence the project that led to the birth of this work.

The paradox

Africa is believed by many to be the richest continent in the world as far as natural resource endowment is concerned. Yet Africa is home to the poorest people on earth. Nigeria, Angola, Algeria and Libya together produce a substantial portion of the world's crude oil. South Africa and several other African countries are a major source of the world's gold output. Botswana, the Democratic Republic of Congo and Sierra Leone are a major source of diamond, and a number of other African countries export such strategic minerals as chrome, bauxite, manganese and uranium in substantial quantities. A good proportion of the world's tropical hardwood, coffee, cocoa and rubber exports are produced in Africa (Legwaila, 2006: 2). For example, Nigeria boasts of world class wealth creating resources. It is the world's ninth largest oil producer and ranks fifth in natural gas reserves. Below ground, there are about forty year's worth of oil and a century's worth of natural gas. Nigeria has a human resource potential of a well trained and frighteningly ambitious humanity. Nigeria has more than four million university trained professionals. They constitute the largest, best trained, most acquisitive black elite on the continent. Yet, despite all this potential, Chinua Achebe, the Nigerian novelist made a seemingly scathing analysis:

> Nigeria is not a great country. It is one of the most disorderly nations in the world. It is one of the most corrupt, insensitive, inefficient places under the sun. It is one of the most expensive countries and one of those that give the least

value for money. It is dirty, callous, noisy, ostentatious, dishonest and vulgar. In short, it is among the most unpleasant places on earth (Harden, 1993: 275 – 276).

People like Martin Luther King and Malcom X died with high hopes about the glorious prospects for Africa. In the words of Malcom X (Haley, 1965:367), "Africa is seething with serious awareness of herself, her wealth, and of her power, and of her destined role in the world". If these people came back to life today, they would be utterly perplexed by the reality on the ground. In short, fifty years later, the hope is less alive.

The key question is: What happened to the momentum and optimism of the early 1960s? Who is profiting and benefiting from all these natural resources and the economic progress Africa has experienced within the last 10 years (The 48 countries of sub-Saharan Africa are enjoying a period of unparalled economic success. Economic growth has reached an average of 6.6 percent (Africa Progress Report, 2008: 3)?

The question can be concretized in one context about Nigeria: The Niger Delta produces the most oil in Nigeria yet its people are among the poorest in Nigeria. Foreign companies take oil wealth to their countries. Stories are rife of a few government officials pocketing the taxes paid and meant to be invested in the community, leaving the local people destitute, consequently, driving the youths to violence. While the oil in the Niger Delta may be a blessing to the foreign companies and those few government officials, it is definitely a curse to the local population. Today the natural resources of Africa and the wealth created from them are largely owned by non-Africans. This and other similar examples elsewhere in Africa, and diverse statistics all point in the same direction, lead us to the daunting question, paradox of sorts: How can the richest continent in the world be home to the poorest people on earth? Even commonsense seems to work against this. Take two people for example, one has a million dollars in a bank account and the other, 10, 000 dollars. How can the one with a million dollars be poorer than that one with 10, 000 dollars? This is the sad truth and paradox about Africa. Africa is the richest continent in terms of natural resource endowment, yet it is home to the poorest people on earth.

I have heard that Africa is an over researched continent but I am not sure if the foregoing questions have been explored enough because if they were, I am sure, the economic situation of Africa would be different. Lack of critical education and capacity is a major plague on the continent. As a result we do not ask ourselves the same type of questions others have asked and answered, in the course, overtaking us by light years. Have we as a people sufficiently engaged on questions about the times we are living in and how we should interpret them? How do we as a people stand economically, politically, culturally and technologically in relation to others and why? What does it take to succeed in this era? How do we define success and what is the success formula others are using that we are not? Who is losing and gaining from our situation? What resources do we have and how can we transform these into our and not other people's wealth? What is unique about Africa and how can we use that uniqueness to our advantage? How can we stop being a burden to others and make ourselves useful to the world? These are the type of questions that after they have been properly answered have moved a people forward.

I was recently asked to speak on African leadership to clients of a global consultancy firm. My simple understanding of leadership is that one is ahead in an aspect of life or some aspects of life and that others are following them as a result. This got me thinking – what is African leadership? Does such a thing exist? In what aspect is Africa ahead? Can Africa claim economic leadership, political leadership, technological leadership? Without fear of contradiction the answer is a definite no.

Through ignorance and manipulation Africa's natural resources continue to be squandered by non-Africans – creating wealth outside the continent and entrenching poverty on the continent. It is a natural law that if you do not know and use what you have, somebody else will and they will do it to their advantage or interest. Looting and pillaging of Africa's natural resources by non-Africans is the major explanation why Africa, the richest continent in the world, is also home to the poorest people. Since this situation has been going on for over five hundred years with increasing gravity, reversing it will take nothing short of a revolution of a magnitude not seen yet on the face of this continent. The situation in Africa is so grave that many leading authorities believe that the continent has reached a tipping point and is beyond redemption and therefore is heading for oblivion (Meredith, 2007: 400). Creating a sense of urgency and the timelessness of the moment, awakening a continental consciousness and building momentum for a revolution like struggle for the economic liberation of the African continent is the goal of this book.

Challenging the African mind

A lot has been written about Africa, especially the history of the continent and the woes and challenges the continent is facing today. Not much, however, has been written about how Africa can catch up economically with the rest of the world. It is also important to note that much of what has been written about Africa is by non-Africans. The history and current situation of Africa has mostly been captured through non-African eyes. I strongly believe that *the sympathizer cannot mourn more than the bereaved* and that *not all sympathizers mean or come to help*. This book therefore aims to make an African contribution to the debate of the African situation. It also hopes to make a contribution to the less discussed debate on how Africa can gain genuine economic independence and determine her own economic destiny. This is obviously an ambitious undertaking and I do not claim to be an in-depth expert on Africa or economic development.

This work is coming out of conviction and a sense of urgency and gravity of the issue under discussion. I am a concerned African who has an opportunity to travel to some African countries in my capacity as a development consultant. I have also had an opportunity to travel and briefly stay in a few countries outside Africa in the same capacity. My aim is to inspire the average African on the continent and outside the continent to rise up and be counted in the struggle for the economic liberation of the continent and its people. In this regard I hope to make this more of an inspirational rather than academic work, although it will definitely make an academic contribution. I therefore do not intend to target any institution or establishment concerned with the development of Africa and the working of those institutions. Instead, I intend to target and challenge the African mind and awaken that mind to the consciousness of its responsibility in the economic liberation of the continent.

Ken Saro Wiwa, a Nigerian with the conscience to liberate Africa from resource exploitation, once said the worst sin on earth is the failure to think. It is thoughtlessness that has reduced Africa to beggardom, to famine, poverty, and disease. The failure to use the creative imagination has reduced Africans to the status of mimic men and consumers of the product of others imagination (Harden, 1993: 277). Embracing creative imagination and thoughtfulness in relation to the economic liberation of the continent is the challenge that the African mind needs to rise up to. This is the way to stop being 'mimic men' and become consumers of our own products and also let others become consumers of products (not only raw materials) of our imagination.

Today a lot of Africans still believe that problems on the continent are caused by the West. Paradoxically, they also believe that the continent's salvation will come from the same West. But five hundred years of waiting should tell us that we may as well wait for another five hundred years before the salvation comes, if ever it will come at all. Economic salvation will come through self effort. Others can help or hinder but the final responsibility lies with the bereaved people not the sympathizers. *The sting of a bed bug can best be described by those in an infested hut*

Napoleon Hill (2004: 47) observed that millions of people believe themselves 'doomed' to poverty and failure because of some strange force over which they believe they have no control. He notes that these people are the creators of their own 'misfortunes' because of this negative belief, which is picked up by the (collective) subconscious mind and translated into its physical equivalent. This observation is true about Africa and Africans. Just as we are creators of our own poverty and 'misfortunes' we can also play creators of our own liberation and economic independence by adopting a positive belief and following it through with constructive action. Those countries that have transformed themselves lifted themselves from the exact situation we are in today and their resolve to succeed and the successes in the end, show that this is not just wishful thinking or some day dreaming, it is a possibility.

Africa's most formidable challenge

The biggest challenge Africa faces today is the fact that the majority of the people on the continent do not know that Africa is not economically independent. They are under the illusion that because we are politically independent then we are also economically independent. Those who know that we are not economically independent choose to ignore or trivialize the fact. Political independence and economic independence are not the same. True independence starts with self-dependence or the ability to exist without depending on others for survival. Political independence without economic independence is meaningless. In fact it is like *banking one's hopes on an unloaded gun*. Just as the first wave for the independence of Africa brought political independence, the next wave should bring economic independence. The magnitude of the struggle will need to be more or less that which brought us political independence. Addressing the deep lack of consciousness and sense of urgency for the need for the struggle for the economic independence of the continent is the burden of this book.

There are two groups of people in Africa. The first group comprises the majority and this is the group that has never known life to be any better. The other group is that of the minority rich. Those in the majority poor lead a life of daily struggle for mere existence and survival. For instance, the African in this category is the lowest paid employee in the world. On the other hand, those minority rich, however, live a standard of life comparable to and in some cases, even better than that lived by their counterparts in the developed parts of the world. Both these situations immobilize action and struggle for continental economic liberation. This is because those struggling with daily existence cannot imagine another and a better life. At the same time, those living in affluence do not feel the pain and may not empathize enough with their unfortunate brothers and sisters. Sometimes one gets the impression that the so-called African leaders belong to the minority haves and have lost their capacity to empathize with the people they are supposed to lead. This book therefore aims to awaken consciousness in both these groups. It aims to ignite a flame of anger that can drive both groups to positive and constructive action.

The framework: the strategic fit model

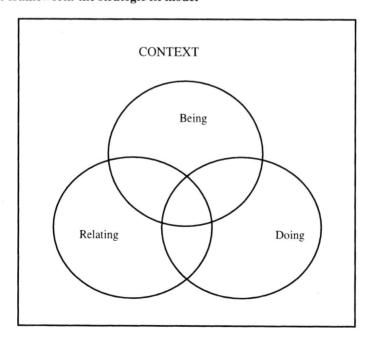

The model illustrates that an entity exists in a context or task environment. The task environment comprises political factors, economic factors, technological factors and socio-cultural factors. Political factors determine an entity's capacity to get what it wants despite resistance from others. Economic factors determine an entity's capacity to create wealth. Technological factors refer to an entity's capacity to create competitive levers. Finally, socio-cultural factors refer to an entity's capacity to preserve and utilize positive aspects of its culture and identity. The task environment offers the entity opportunities to seize and threats to mitigate. This would help us understand what opportunities the continent has and how to seize them. It would also help understand the threats the continent is facing and how to mitigate them.

The *being* of the entity refers to the constituent elements of the entity. These (from visible to invisible aspects) include: the entity's financial and material resources, skills and competences; policies, systems and procedures; structure, strategies, leadership (vision and mission); and values.

The *doing* of the continent refers to its understanding and practice of leverage activities – or its understanding of its niche and how to build power based on the identified niche. Without a niche development of power is not possible.

The *relating* of the entity refers to its ability to engage in collaboration and cooperation that result in synergy or at least in the benefit of the entity.

A proper balance of the entity's *being*, *doing* and *relating* results is the entity's strategic fit with its task environment. Strategic fit refers to a strategically positioned entity that is able to exploit or seize opportunities and manage threats in its task environment. In short, a strategically positioned entity is able to determine its own destiny or create the future it wants.

The organization of the book
Based on the strategic fit model above, the book is divided into ten chapters as follows:

- This first chapter introduces the strategic fit model upon which the subsequent chapters of the book are based.
- The second chapter discusses the nature of the struggle for the economic liberation of Africa.
- The third chapter discusses Africa's economy in contrast to other economies.
- The fourth chapter discusses Africa's politics and their effect on economic development on the continent.
- The fifth chapter discusses the role of civil society and civil society organizations in the struggle for the economic independence of Africa.
- The sixth chapter discusses African culture in the modern world and how it is affecting the continent's economic development as a response to the opportunities and threats identified in the foregoing chapters.
- The seventh chapter discusses South Korea's economic miracle and draws some lessons Africa can learn from that experience.

- The eighth chapter discusses what Africa should be, do and how it should relate within the continent and with others outside the continent.
- The ninth chapter paints a picture of what an economically liberated Africa would or should look like.
- The last chapter concludes the book by outlining concrete suggestions on how Africa and Africans can liberate themselves economically.

The essence of the book

In this struggle for the continent's economic independence, the first step is for people to be convinced beyond any shadow of doubt that Africa is not economically independent. It must be firmly established and entrenched in peoples' hearts that the founding fathers got political and not economic independence and that economic independence is a mission yet to be accomplished with at least the same intensity as that of the political struggle.

Just as before the 1960's much of Africa was not politically independent, today's Africa is not economically independent. Just as each of the countries on the continent commemorates political independence on their respective special days there also will be need in the near future for each of the countries and eventually the continent to gain and celebrate economic independence on their respective special days. The economic Independence Days will need to be celebrated each year on days different from the days we celebrate political independence days to signify the shift from political to economic independence. It is my most sincere prayer that this will begin to become a reality in my own life time. This is not merely some wishful thinking. In December 2008, China celebrated 30 years of the launch of economic reforms initiated by President Deng Xiaoping.

The type of crisis in Africa sometimes brings forth a great leader. Understandably one such great leader on the continent has been Nelson Mandela. But Mandela has mostly been a political leader. There is need for another leader or leaders of his stature who are economic leaders. Mandela himself said at his ninetieth birthday celebration at Hyde Park, "After almost ninety years of life, it is time for new hands to lift the burden". There is need for new economic leaders to lift the continent out of economic destitution.

Economic independence can be easily explained in very simple terms. A family that does not have its own money but depends on alms and handouts from others is not financially independent. It is a beggar family. Similarly a nation that cannot finance its own national budget but has to depend on others to finance it is a beggar nation. Similarly too, a continent that cannot economically support itself is a beggar continent. It is not economically independent. *When one begs for water it does not quench thirst.*

The essence of the book therefore is that for every African at whatever stage of their development, every decision they make must be guided by the principle question: *How does this decision or act contribute or undermine the struggle for the economic liberation of my family, community, country and continent?* This will require the capacity to acknowledge, confront and change deeply held patterns of thinking and behaving. This understandably is a far much difficult process, and bringing about this fundamental change is the burden of this book. Beyond being convinced that Africa is not economically independent, the most important thing is corrective action. Martin Luther King Jr. emphasizes this point well when he observes,

> Human progress is neither automatic nor inevitable...even a superficial look at history reveals that no social (and economic) advance rolls in on the wheels of inevitability; it comes through the tireless efforts and persistent work of dedicated individuals. Without this hard work, time itself becomes an ally of the primitive forces of irrational emotionalism and social stagnation. We have already suffered unnecessary delays in the civil rights (and economic independence) struggle because of this lack of vigorous and positive action...we cannot wait for a deliverance to come from others moved by their pity for us (Washington, 1991: 104).

CHAPTER 2: THE NATURE OF THE STRUGGLE

Introduction

The story of economic independence cannot be separated from the story of globalization.

Globalization is shifting power away from governments responsible for public good and toward a handful corporations and financial institutions driven by a single imperative - the quest for short term financial gain. This has concentrated massive economic and financial power in the hands of an elite few (Korten, 1995: 12). It is these few people who are benefiting from globalization while the rest of the people are being driven further and further towards starvation and violence, homelessness and beggarly, refugee camps and becoming welfare recipients. Making the world a better place is not part of the conscious agenda of globalization.

Only economically independent countries have a chance to take advantage of the opportunities of globalization while economically dependent countries lack the pre-requisites to enable them participate fully and take advantage of globalization. Globalization refers to growing economic interdependence among countries as reflected in increasing cross-border flows of 3 types of entities: goods and services, capital and know-how (Govindarajan and Gupta, 2001: 4). Some of the key indicators that can be used to measure a country's level of globalization include exports as a ratio of GDP, inward and outward flows of both foreign direct investment and portfolio investment, and inward and outward flows of royalty payments associated with technology transfer. By these measures most sub-Saharan Africans remain beyond the reach of all global economic progress (Shapiro, 2008: 84).

They remain beyond the reach of economic progress because they have generally failed to take advantage of the forces driving globalization and its benefits for those who are ready for them. These forces include: an ever increasing number of countries embracing the free market ideology, the continuing onward march of technological advances, the shifting of the economic center of gravity from the developed to the developing countries especially those in Asia; and the increasing opportunities arising from the emerging borderless economy.

The cost to pay for failing to rising up to the challenge of globalization is increasing marginalization and destitution of the masses on the continent. The opportunities of globalization can drive development and the threats can thwart it. The latter is the case in most of Africa.

The African challenge

Development makes meaning when we are able to spread the good things we have in the city centers to rural areas where most of the people in Africa live. This is a true measure of development. The problem of rapid urbanization in Africa is an indication of the worsening living conditions in the rural areas. People may know the type of risk they are taking to come to town when they have no foundation or preparation for making a meaningful living there but they feel that is a better risk than staying back in the rural communities. An African proverb says *when you see a rat running into the fire, what it is running away from is hotter than the fire.* When people run to stay in town, it means that what they are running away from in the rural community is hotter than the problems they anticipate in town. A meaningful way to address the problem of rapid urbanization is to make available in their own rural areas what they are looking for in town. This is the nature of the struggle in the economic liberation of Africa.

I would want to present a picture of a typical African rural community. Instead of presenting a grand picture of the situation on the continent, I will present a picture of a typical African community. I will present a picture of a typical African community because that is where the common person for whom this book is meant lives; and that is where the effectiveness of all change efforts is finally measured; and that is where success or failure of such changes are most and realistically visible. Mahatma Gandhi clearly stated that the village or the community is the locus of the direct struggle against misery and the proper organizational level of direct democracy and socio-economic life. He also observed that the exploitation of the village is the common deed of foreign imperialism and its local brokers – the local town dwellers (Sachs, 1980: 49). When a critical number of communities on the continent changes, the country changes and eventually the continent will change.

For most poor people economic growth measures such as Gross National Product (GNP), Gross Domestic Product (GDP) and per capita income have no meaning or worth because they do not say much about what is happening at grassroots level especially among the poor people. When people are told that their country's economies are growing they are often confused because personally they may not see any positive changes. Sometimes their own lives are getting worse with increasing costs of food, rent and other basic necessities. So while generally economic growth has been increasing in Africa since 1994 by up to 6.6 percent per year on average (Africa Progress Panel, 2008: 5), this has not always matched improvement in people's lives. It is common knowledge that economic growth often brings social decline in its wake.

We need a concise and vivid description of the current situation in order to incite pain and anger that can drive people to action and constructive action for that matter. As a development worker, I have observed that we rarely help people to understand the gravity of their situation through reflection and helping compare themselves with people lived in similar predicaments but have managed to lift themselves out of economic dependence. *A problem clearly defined is a problem half solved.*

The typical African community

The typical African community is one that represents total dependence. It represents economic, political, technological, cultural and spiritual dependence. It is to these facets that we now turn.

The economy of the typical African community

There is not enough food for every household in the community throughout the year. If the food is available it is of low quality or of low nutritional value. The people are not able to produce the food themselves or they cannot afford to buy in needed quantities and quality. Fending for food still remains a major preoccupation to which most of the people's energy goes. Politicians are still using food as a political tool to manipulate the people in their favor. Women and girls have to walk very long distances to fetch water. The safety of the water is not guaranteed. Getting access to improved sanitation and sewerage systems is still a big challenge. Some people are still practicing 'open defecation'. Surroundings are not clean and hygienic.

There is no health center in the community. If it is there, there are inadequate qualified personnel. If the personnel are there, you will be very lucky if there are any drugs in the health center. People have to spend the whole day in a queue only to be told to come again the following day because the doctor could not see them that day because there were too many people in the queue.

There is no ambulance at the health center. If it is there, it is not in a running condition. One is very unfortunate to get sick in such a community because there is no guarantee that they will be transferred to a referral hospital. Many people are still dying unnecessary deaths because they cannot make it to the hospital in time.

The community is inaccessible especially during rainy seasons. The community is isolated from the major road networks. Young people from the community staying in town or outside the country have to think twice before visiting parents and relatives in the community because they wonder whether their cars will reach their homes and if they do whether their cars will be able to drive out of the communities due to the poor condition of the roads.

The huts in which the people live are a health hazard. They are usually small and do no have enough space for all the people living in them. They are poorly ventilated, poorly thatched such that they leak when it rains. People sleep on a reed mat not on a bed. A mattress is a 'luxury' they cannot afford. The houses are usually infested with bed bugs, lice, rats and cockroaches. The people cannot afford good clothes. The best they can afford is second hand clothes thrown away in Europe and America. Most of them cannot afford shoes. They walk barefoot and therefore one can still find people with cracked feet infested with jigger fleas.

Children in the community find it very hard to attend school. There are no role models that the children can point at as evidence of the importance of going to school. Some parents have to be coerced to send their children to school because the importance of school is not obvious to everyone in the community. The schools have dilapidated class rooms and facilities. Some children are still learning under trees. There are hardly any improved water and sanitation facilities at each school. The pupil-teacher ratio could be the highest in the world. The schools are so far away and apart that children sometimes have to wait another five years to be old enough to walk the long distances to school. The streets to and from schools are not safe for the children. Children are being assaulted on their way to and from school. When they arrive at the school they are too tired to concentrate.

People in the communities have to travel long distances to find basic commodities. The prices of basic commodities in the rural areas where people are poorer are much higher than those in town. Even in the rural areas, the people supplying these basic needs in a more organized way are not the community members themselves or some Africans. They are people of other races.

Usually the community does not produce anything. If they produce some produce or product there is no ready or profitable market. Everyone is working in isolation. There are no cooperatives to effect economies of scale and ensure synergy and to also increase bargaining power. Greedy middle men are still exploiting the community. Most people in the community cannot read, write and count and therefore cannot participate meaningfully in community life.

In short the people in the community do not have control over their resources and they are not turning these resources into wealth. The people, especially the youths are not gainfully employed. Most people are idle (not lazy). The community is not attractive enough to prevent youths from unnecessary emigration.

The politics of a typical African community

The political leaders of the community are not democratically elected. They are not elected to the satisfaction of both the winners and losers. Rigging is expected and accepted. The leaders are not elected based on merit but party and tribal loyalty. The leaders are masters of the people. They represent their own will and values and not those of the people. The leaders are elected not from among the people. They do not stay in the community together with the people. They stay in town and only show up when election dates approach. The leaders being masters of the people do not have to be held accountable. They do not account for their decisions and actions and the people cannot make legitimate claims and demands on the leaders. In general, the community takes an accepting and not a questioning stance. Political leaders still believe in ruling for life. Term limits are not respected. There are no effective succession plans leading, many times, to frequent cycles of 'mountains and valleys' as good leaders are followed by bad leaders and bad leaders are followed by good leaders. The process is mostly by chance rather than by design as there are no proper succession plans. When the president of Guinea-Conakry, Lasana Conte died in Dec 2008, after being in power for 24 years, the military immediately took over power an indicator of lack of any transition plan for smooth transfer of power. Lasana Conte himself took power through a coup on the justification and promise that he would change the lives of the people and eliminate the corruption of the government he overthrew. About twenty-four years later the people were disillusioned and gladly accepted the military junta who had taken over power hoping that they would be different. The story of hope and disillusionment is the norm in many African countries and communities.

Diversity is taken as rebellion and it is discouraged and punished. Any one with a different opinion is an enemy and they have to be cast out. The leaders are feared rather than respected.

No one's security is guaranteed. People are taking security into their own hands because the government system has failed them. Known criminals walk free on the roads when people with lesser crimes or no crimes at all are languishing in jails. Some people are above the law. People are still being abducted, imprisoned or even killed for having different political views. People are still detained for long periods without trial.

The technology of a typical African community
The community has no telephone services. If there are any phones, they do not work or are not affordable. It costs one the earth to make a simple phone call. Phones are used only to send funeral and crisis messages because they are too expensive. Cell phones do not work because there is no network. Access to the internet for business opportunities is a far fetched dream. If by some rare chance it happens to be there, it takes the whole day to connect. There is no resource center or library which stocks relevant materials – information and knowledge that can help the community members turn their resources into wealth. After all not many people know how to read or write. The radio is still used as tool for propaganda with the aim of controlling the people's thinking and manipulating them to think in a certain way. It is not used as tool for economic empowerment.

People are still using firewood and charcoal for fuel. They have no access to electricity. If by some chance electricity is available, black outs are the norm. If they have electricity for an entire week without a black out people are surprised. Both the firewood and charcoal are becoming more and more expensive as their stocks are fast running out.

Because of the bad roads, one has to walk very long distances to be able to get public transport. The private vehicles that brave the bad roads are very expensive. The soils have been so depreciated that without inorganic inputs no crop can grow and yet the prices of the inorganic inputs are way beyond the reach of the people in the community. Only those who get remittances from their children in town can afford the inorganic inputs like fertilizers.

The culture of a typical African community
The culture of the African community is being turned up side down. The principle feature of the community is that people and relationships are more important than things, there is sharing of collective ownership of opportunities, responsibilities and challenges. There is participatory decision making and leadership, loyalty and patriotism, and reconciliation as a goal of conflict management. Increasing reversals in the foregoing principles is more of the norm today.

Elderly people have no place in the community. They are seen more as a burden than anything else. The role of elderly members of the community as custodians of culture and wisdom is being lost. Elderly people are not respected and consulted for their wisdom. Many of the elderly people themselves do not demonstrate the capacity to play the roles expected of them. The proverb *the death of an old person is like an entire library burnt* is under question.

Parenting has become an individual or individual family responsibility and the differences in the worlds of the parents and their children are making it very difficult for the parents to offer proper guidance to the children. In fact many parents have lost control of their children. Rituals that were meant to 'educate' children about their new responsibilities as they reach particular stages in life are ridiculed as primitive and not 'cool' for the new generation. Systems for collective parenting, a key African feature in raising up children, have fallen apart in the name of modernity.

Parents are proud that their children cannot speak their own languages very well and that they speak English or French better. For those who went to school, conversations in their homes are held in English. Children are whipped for speaking their mother tongue in the home.

Conclusion

The typical African community is one in which people are dependent. They are dependent economically, socio-culturally, technologically and spiritually. They cannot therefore exert economic, political, socio-cultural and spiritual influence on the nation and the continent. Turning this situation around is the nature of the struggle. Fifty years after 'independence' how can this still be? Many Africans have lost faith in themselves and have come to believe that where they are economically is where they are supposed to be – less than every other group in the world. This is reflected in the apathy and lack of attitude or determination to fight or reverse the situation as in the words of one participant in a discussion on how to resolve Africa's problems,

> What should be our African response? I am confused. The issues are so complicated. I do not know how to respond or to interpret what is happening because I am part of the problem. I benefit from the system that is creating poverty to my people. I may be secure but what about my children and their future. My country is so poor no one is listening any more... when I go home from here I will find people queuing on my door begging for money. People are so poor, it is very depressing, and I just wish I went back to the 1970s when life was so good.

Castro (2007: 399) rightly observes when he says,

> Today, no task is more urgent than creating universal awareness, taking the problem to the masses, to the billions of men and women of every age including children who inhabit the planet. The objective conditions, the sufferings of the immense majority of those people create the subjective conditions for the task of awareness building. Everything is related: illiteracy, unemployment, poverty, hunger, illness, and disease, lack of drinking water, housing, electricity, desertification, climate change, disappearance of forests, floods, hurricanes, droughts, erosion, biodiversity loss, plagues and tragedies".

The fundamental root cause, at least for Africa lies in her lack of economic independence and therefore inability to determine her own destiny and lack of power to influence other key players on how to govern the world in a way that there would be utopia for everyone without harming the foundation upon which that utopia is built.

Gandhi's statement that some people are so poor that to them God can only appear in the form of bread is true for most of the above mentioned communities. This happening after sixty years of incessant donor aid and other similar strategies makes a very strong negative statement about those strategies.

All the above said characteristics are just symptoms of the real problem. *If you cut a piece of a liana creeper without removing the roots, it will continue to creep.* The root of the problem is the continent's lack of economic independence resulting from the continent's failure to turn its resources into wealth.

CHAPTER 3: AFRICA'S ECONOMY

Why is Africa home to the poorest people on earth?

One of the greatest paradoxes in the world today is of Africa being the richest continent in terms of natural resource endowment yet being home to the poorest people on earth. Kwame Nkrumah once said the DRC alone can potentially produce enough food to feed the whole of Africa with surplus for export and yet Africa is a net importer of food and home to the largest number of malnourished children. It is a perpetual recipient of relief items.

Africa contains in excess of 40% the world's natural resources and yet these do not currently benefit the Africans as much as they do other groups of people. The issue of Africa being the richest continent on earth in terms of natural resource endowment is well documented and I do not wish to belabor myself with unnecessary repetition. What I intend to focus on is why Africa is home to the poorest people on earth yet it is the richest continent. I have only one explanation for this. *Africa is the richest continent on earth and at the same time home to the poorest people because it has failed to transform its natural resources into wealth.* Landes (2001: 269) emphasizes this point well when he says that it is not lack of money (resources) that holds development. The biggest impediment to development is social, cultural and technological unreadiness – lack of knowledge and technical know how. In other words, lack of ability to use money or resources.

The natural resources themselves are not wealth. They are potential wealth. There is need for skill and capacity to transform the resources into wealth. In their raw form they are useless and at least not worth enough to create wealth. The challenge in breaking the poverty cycle is to transform resources into own and not other people's wealth.

Will aid develop Africa?

In basic economics we learn that the factors of production are land, labor, capital and management. The key word is production – production of wealth. As Africans we have a lot of land (natural resources), and labor. What we do not have is capital (because we do not own anything). We do not have capital because our economies are donor dependent. Donors being smart people are not keen to support us in such a way that we will reach a stage where we will not need them. They may not support us in such a way that they think may hurt them in future. It is said, *"If you want your domestic worker to continue slaving for you, then control his poverty"* What this means simply is that we should not expect aid in its present form to bring about economic development to Africa. Aid will bring what aid can bring – relief and not development. It is a rule of life that development is always endogenous. Development always comes from within and not without. Personal development is always self development. Community development is the particular community's responsibility. Organization development is the particular organization's responsibility. National development is national responsibility. All development is self development. No person can develop another and no country can develop another. Others can only assist or hinder. *The sympathizer cannot mourn more than the bereaved.*

When there is a crisis in the world, Africa will always be the worst hit. HIV and AIDS, rising costs of food and fuel, climate change, bird flu, swine flu and any other natural or man made calamity will hit Africa the worst because the so-called donor countries will just reduce their aid to take care of these problems in their countries first. No one wants to die on behalf of another. In fact the logic is you can only love your neighbor after you have loved yourself first. They have to be alive before they can help us. This is why they will take care of themselves first. I remember fighting for change within an organization that I was working for at one time. We fought so hard because we believed that the organization needed to be run and managed in a different way. The fight kept dragging until we realized that we could not change the organization because it was their organization and not ours. The donors and expatriates apparently had a clear agenda that they were pursuing which was not as clear to us and they were not going to change simply because we wanted them to. It was then that I decided that the change we were seeking or looking for could only be possible in an organization that was our own. Fortunately or unfortunately, we got fired from the organization which gave us the opportunity to start our own organization.

It is very clear now that much of the aid business is not so much about poverty reduction as it is about geopolitics. The poorest places on earth do not have the highest concentration of aid and the only hope for these places is to realize that they are alone. Help is not on the way. They have to do something for themselves or wait to go into oblivion.

The issue about aid is how it is helping us to accumulate capital so that we can put our land (natural resources) and labor to work in the process of creating wealth. Aid that does not contribute towards capital creation is detrimental to the continent's economic development. There is therefore only one criterion for assessing the genuineness of aid's developmental motives: how is this aid contributing towards the creation of capital? If it is not, that is bad aid aimed at further domesticating the continent.

Transforming our resources into wealth also implies moving beyond aid to trade. There is no continent or country in this world that was developed by aid. The best aid can do is to help the continent develop its capital so that the country or continent can become an equal player in the world. Transforming resources into wealth is an arena of trade not aid. This is because in the real world no one is willing to give away part of their wealth to another group. Each group has to create its own wealth. The way to create wealth is through trade and trade is competition. This is why the more advanced economies of the world will resist with all their might to open up their markets to fair trade. They have a position of privilege through which they control the world and they will not easily give it away. It is naïve to expect that they will. They worked so hard to reach where they are and they will not give it away just like that. They earned that position and anyone who wants to play at the same level must earn their positions as well. This is what China and India have done. This is what Africa must do.

These countries did not arrive at their current positions by fighting for fairer markets alone. They created their own wealth and rose to the position where they are today.

These countries did not arrive where they are today by aid (though aid may have played its appropriate role). I remember one time listening to the radio and there was a report that India refused to get some aid money from America and suggested instead that the money be given to some country needing aid more in Africa.

Aid is a sign of lack of economic independence. Having one's debts canceled is a sign of utter destitution. To a normal mind therefore aid and debt cancellation are not issues to celebrate about. A key concern to any normal mind who find themselves where they have to live by aid and need to have their debts canceled is to feel sorry for oneself, repent and try to get out of the situation as fast as possible. Living by aid and having one's debts canceled signifies a loss of one's dignity as a man or a woman. A family that has to live on aid and has to have its debts canceled is a sorry sight.

I do not think the foregoing sentiments should be different for a country or an entire continent. Africa's dependence on aid for its survival is a sign of its lack of economic independence. Its celebration for having its debts canceled is a sign of its utter destitution. The abnormal thing is that Africa cries for more aid (with no end to aid dependence in sight) and celebrates its debt cancellations. There is no urgency in the countries or on the continent to get out of the sad and sorry state at all. The issue of the country's or the continent's dignity in the eyes of the rest of the world does not arise at all.

After fifty years of political independence and donor aid today Africa remains the world's poorest continent. In this book I argue that Africa remains the poorest continent in the world because it took a 'begging bowl' or 'aid based' approach to development in contrast to the Asian countries like Singapore, South Korea, Taiwan and Hong Kong who took a 'trade approach' to development. Today it is clear that the Asian countries were wiser in their choice as they have managed to conquer and make poverty history at least at the levels that poverty exists in Africa. They have managed to become economically independent a dream that Africa has not yet started dreaming.

To turn our back from oblivion and begin to walk consciously towards utopia I am suggesting that Africa needs to work out a strategy that will enable her to eventually throw away the crutches of aid and begin to walk on her own feet by creating her own wealth and thus gain economic independence. Just as China was the 'sleeping giant' a hundred years ago, today's sleeping giant is Africa. In this book I am striving to show why and how the African sleeping giant can wake up and make herself economically independent and take her rightful strategic role in the world.

Landes (2001: 523) emphasizes that,

"History tells us that the most successful cures of poverty come from within.
Foreign aid can help, but like windfall wealth, can also hurt. It can discourage
effort, and plant a crippling sense of incapacity. The hand that receives is

always under the one that gives. No, what counts is work, thrift, honesty, patience, tenacity . . . at bottom, no empowerment is so effective as self-empowerment".

The need for genuine aid

Social development is primarily the work of government. Economic development is primarily the work of entrepreneurs and business people. The entrepreneur develops ideas that business people turn into wealth. The government uses the taxes from the business people to facilitate social development. The government achieves social development through responsive governance, socially friendly economic policies and universal provision of social services (Mehrotra and Jolly, 1998: 432). Civil society is supposed to hold government accountable in making sure it is fulfilling the foregoing responsibilities. Civil society is also supposed to hold businesses accountable in making sure that their profit motive is not being pursued at the expense of poor people's political, social and economic rights.

In this case, economic independence is a product of wealth-creating ideas, vibrant businesses (who invest in the economy in which they are operating and not only siphoning resources and wealth out of the country to their own countries), effective governments and a vibrant civil society. A government that gets its own money from its business people and entrepreneurs is an economically independent government and that country is an economically independent country. That country has genuine sovereignty and it is truly sovereign. When aid replaces the entrepreneurs and businesses as the engine for driving a country economically, that country is not economically independent for the simple reason that it is dependent on outsiders as it is not self reliant. That country's genuine sovereignty and autonomy are compromised. That country is under obligation to follow the donors' agenda because *he who pays the piper determines the tune*. It is as simple as that.

Donors can only make a contribution towards the continent's economic independence if their funding is invested not only on social services through governments but more importantly if their funding is invested in strengthening local entrepreneurship and businesses and lifting them to compete favorably at the world stage. Much of the current donor funding goes to governments in the so-called budgetary support mechanisms and civil society organizations. Hardly does any funding in any significant levels go to supporting or building entrepreneurial or business power on the continent. We all have seen how Western governments have been very quick to bail out their failed businesses. Why did they do this? It is because they know that government on its own cannot create wealth. Governments only distribute wealth that has already been created by businesses. It is because they know that civil society does not produce wealth. Civil society waits for citizens and the government to give them money which the government itself gets from the taxes of the businesses. Western governments are quick to bail out failed businesses because they know that any weakness in business power signals loss of economic independence.

African businesses, which are more conspicuous by their absence than presence, have always needed *'more bailing out'* but no one has come to their rescue at least at the level Western governments have done to their businesses. Currently African businesses cannot be bailed out by their governments because their governments do not have the type of money that can make the needed shift as we have seen in the Western countries. They can only be bailed out by donors if the donors are serious about Africa's economic independence and *'working themselves out of the job'*. The big push initiative by Tony Blair was aimed at raising $500 billion to finally lift Africa out of poverty. We all celebrated and hoped that if such an amount of money was raised we would make poverty history on the continent. But we are surprised that the government of America spent $700 billion to bail out just one sector of its economy, the financial institutions and that some quarters feel that the money invested in bailing out that sector is not sufficient. If just one sector in one country needs that amount of money, what would an entire continent like Africa need? If we are serious about creating utopia and avoiding oblivion in Africa and if donors are serious about demonstrating the genuineness of the aid motives there is great and urgent need to *'bail out'* the African business sector. As the Americans would say there is need to *put the money where the mouth is.* According to Oxfam, $580 billion is enough to act as a stimulus to the whole continent of Africa if this money is invested in fiscal discipline, developmental aid and improving infrastructure.

The need for donors to invest in the African business sector also derives from the fact that African markets are too small to allow their firms to grow big enough to become their countries' economic engines by becoming world competitors. If the firms cannot become world competitors and thus bring wealth from outside the countries' and the continent they cannot become engines driving economic progress and their countries will have to continue depending on donor aid and relief.

At a recent international conference I met an official from one of the largest international donor agencies. He told me that he was a budget holder of $250 million per year. He said that his problem was that he was confused because similar amounts given in aid in the past only produced negligible results. He was wondering where to spend or give the money so that it could make the most difference. Unfortunately, I did not have a clear answer at that time. I had not done my own reflection to be able to provide useful guidance. But If I were asked the same question today, I would tell him to allocate the money in equal proportions to deserving civil society organizations, governments and business organizations or organizations dedicated to building entrepreneurial and business power on the continent. The three together will create the conditions for economic independence and eventually relieve him and his organization from their aid burden. Unfortunately he went back from the conference convinced that he had found the answer to his confusion and that was to spend that money on civil society organizations as 'this would empower them to hold their governments accountable'.

The foregoing incident reminded me of an evaluation I did for one of the partner civil society organization. This particular client has shifted from providing direct services to communities to 'empowering' the communities to demand their economic rights from the government through what they called a 'citizenship program' using a rights based approach. They stopped calling the communities, communities and now they are referred to as 'rights holders'. The government and other institutions are now called 'duty bearers'. The 'citizenship program' is almost backfiring. One of the respondents I interviewed put it well when she said,

> We liked the way they worked with us before when they were providing basic services like water, agricultural inputs and others. They even built schools, clinics and bridges in our communities. But now they are saying their role is to empower us to demand the same services from the government when they and us know very well that the government does not have the capacity to deliver the services that they were delivering because the government does not have as much money as they do. They spend $20,000 to teach and mobilize us to demand a $1,000 service or rights as they call them from the district assembly which the district assembly does not have and we all know it is true that they don't have the $1,000.

The governments cannot give what they do not have no matter how civil society organizations empower the citizens to demand those rights. This emphasizes the need to balance strengthening both civil society and governments so that governments can justifiably be expected to be responsive to 'rights holders'. This is why governments need genuine aid to be able to be responsive to the needs of the rights holders and not to be manipulated to serve donor agendas only. The government would actually get more autonomy if they got their money from the taxes of business because with this money they only have their own and not other people's agenda to follow.

All this said, it is important to repeat and emphasize that Africa cannot bank on others for its economic independence. It is very unlikely that others will be wailing to *'bail out'* the African business sector as they have done with their own businesses. It is also likely that aid will continue to be invested in social and not economic development initiatives that can eventually make the continent economically independent. The implication of this is that economic independence for the continent is essentially an African responsibility. This is expected because independence, true independence is not given. It is not given on a silver platter. It must be demanded and many times fought for. Economic independence can only be fought for from 'within ourselves' because we can only be our own liberators. We can be our own liberators by recognizing our potential and cultivating it into wealth. In short we can be our own liberators by identifying and cultivating a niche in the world and of course, by lobbying for our economic right to get financial support from the donors.

In practical terms, Africa Progress Panel (2008: 5) argues for better quantity and quality aid to Africa that would be characterized by:

- Donors, especially the G8, making funding sources and timetables available in a timely manner, along with stated pledges. Each member country should provide a detailed outline on the potential and availability of funding as well as how funds will be delivered for stated pledges.

- The proportion of aid that is tied must be clearly identified by every member of the G8 and must decrease over time.
- The G8 must take steps to reduce the volatility of aid, and support innovative efforts like the ones suggested above to improve aid quality. Providing information on forthcoming aid disbursements in a timely manner will help reduce volatility, as will commitments that are made over a multi-year time horizon
- In light of existing pledges as well as the need for additional resources to address the food crisis and the problems of climate change, the G8 should renew its discussion on innovative financing mechanisms.

Some people have written very strongly against aid and are calling for its immediate cessation (Hancok, 2004: 192 – 193). This is mostly based on the frustrating and disappointing results from the aid. Unfortunately, these people do not offer a clear, practical and realistic alternative to the current aid system. You do not tell a person hanging on both hands on a branch in a tree to first cease the hanging for him or her to shift to another branch. It makes sense when you show them which branch to shift to, and then the order of actions: carefully take one hand to that new branch, then the other, and finally, carefully lift one leg at a time until the whole body perches on that new branch. The absence of the direction and demonstration can surely result in a dramatic fall. Currently Africa is hanging on a branch of aid. There is a need to shift to the branch of trade. In managing the transition we cannot immediately do away with aid but the nature of the aid needs to change so that it becomes facilitative to the transition and not a hindrance. This means, among other things, the aid should have less strings attached to it in the same sense that *when you give someone a goat, the giving will not become complete and feasible unless you also give that one a rope for tethering that goat.*

The need for Africa to find her niche in the world

Transforming resources into wealth is through trade not aid. It is through transforming raw materials into finished products and services that people from other continents can buy. This is the only known way of bringing about economic development or wealth to a continent or a country. But today Africa has no capacity to take some raw material and or an idea and process it up to the world market as a finished product at least in significant numbers or magnitude worth translating them into wealth.

I personally have no problem with other people like the Chinese, Japanese and American flooding Africa with their finished products and with us consuming these products and services (as long as we are wise consumers which is a big challenge itself). My greatest problem is the failure of Africa to produce its own products and services that others can queue to buy. This brings us to the issue of comparative and competitive advantage. If the Japanese are comparatively and competitively better positioned to produce technological gadgets, if the Americans are better positioned to export beer it is alright. The question is, What is our comparative and competitive advantage that can enable us to export finished products. What is our niche in this world? What finished products or services shall be needed? If we buy technological gadgets from Japan what are we exporting to Japan that the Japanese need from us and will queue to buy? A country or continent without a niche will eventually be written off and sink into oblivion.

Money is not a problem and has never been one. What we have in Africa is an ideas problem – that ability to create million dollar and billion dollar ideas and processing them from concept right through to the world market. There is too much money lying in abundance waiting for useful outlets which can only be created by wealth-creating ideas and knowledge. Genuinely powerful ideas are irresistible no matter their places of origin. Ralph Waldo Emerson said if a person can write a better book, or preach a better sermon, or make a better mouse trap, even if he or she builds his or her house in the woods, the world will make a beaten path to their door.

The key lever to wealth creation: knowledge and brain power
The other issue is, if they need our resources to create what they sell back to us why can't we create those products and services and make them available to our people at more affordable prices and export finished products and services to the world? This brings us to the issue of the key source of wealth today: knowledge and brain power. In the words of Thomas Stewart:

> Growing around us is a new information age economy whose fundamental sources of wealth are knowledge and information rather than natural resources and physical labor. Managing information, finding and growing intellectual capital, storing it, selling it has become the most important task of individuals, businesses and nations (Stewart, 1997: 12).

The greatest advantage the other groups have over Africa and Africans is the knowledge they have and their ability to use that knowledge to transform resources into wealth. And this is a paradox because African intellectuals have gone to the same schools with the other groups and have the same qualifications. The difference is that these people are able to use their degrees to create solutions and wealth for their continents while Africans do not. Africans use their degrees to add titles to their names and get better jobs for themselves. I know of situations where civil servants nearing retirement are sent to study for higher degrees so that they can retire at a higher grade so that they can get a higher pension.

The above issue is also pointing out to the fact that education or qualifications themselves are not enough to guarantee one or a people wealth-creating knowledge or capacity. Formal education is supposed to be a means towards an end and not and end in itself which seems to be the case with most Africans. Most Africans do not subscribe to any journals in their professions except for academic or job related purposes and not self or professional development purposes. I remember a colleague during our graduating days from college, saying he was now free from reading and to demonstrate the magnitude of this freedom, he vowed to go out and burn all his notebooks and books.

Continuous wealth creation is not possible at all levels without reading the best and most relevant information, signing up for specialized classes regularly and hiring the best coaches and mentors one can afford. In the real world, these practices differentiate individuals with similar qualifications – from those who succeed and those who do not.

What is the knowledge that others have to produce what they are producing? What is the knowledge behind their products and services? It is this knowledge that differentiates them from us economically. And it is knowledge that is the lever that equalizes the global economic playground.

One of the major explanations for Africa's poor economic situation therefore is poor knowledge management. The first point in knowledge management is to identify what could be our niche as nations and as a continent. When we identify this niche the second stage is to ask ourselves: What is the knowledge we need in order to create world class services or products in that niche? We then need to ask ourselves another question: What is the knowledge that we already have within our people and how can we download this knowledge from people's heads and package it in usable and easily accessible forms? Lastly, what gaps still exist in the knowledge our people have and then where and how can we get the most relevant knowledge to bridge the gap?

We must use the same methods others have used to get the knowledge they need to be where they are. In the information age much of the knowledge that the continent will need is already available and it is a paradox that relevant information continues to be a very rare resource in much of Africa and that we still have to wait for other people to create that information and knowledge for us. It is a paradox that I will get more information about my country in a British or American library for example than in my own country. Go to any bookshop or library and check the section on Africa. The books will have more European or American authors than African authors. One of the biggest needs of Africa is authors who can address issues and write in a language that people on the continent understand. One of the greatest needs in improving Africa's economy today is investing in think-tanks that specialize in knowledge management or the use of knowledge as a key economic lever.

In summary, knowledge creation is based on utilization of information. We need to develop the capacity to translate information into knowledge and then wealth. Wealth creation is not accidental. It is based on information. More than once I have heard some people saying they were poor until they read such and such a book. They will say I was very fortunate to read that book, I reflected on it, digested it, got the essence of the message and then caught the vision of the author and then my eyes got opened. When I applied its message my life changed. Most of us will read the best inspirational books and listen to the best inspirational speakers. All we achieve is inspiration and nothing more. Do we have capacity to read a book like Napoleon Hill's *Think and Grow Rich* and truly think and grow rich in practice? Through this book Mr Napoleon Hill has been christened the king maker of millionaires. Can we read a book like *The*

Richest Man in Babylon and put its message into practice in our lives? The formula to get rich is now an open secret but we still cannot see it. There is even a book entitled, *The Secret* but we will read it and still not see the secret to wealth creation. Any person who does not read cannot lead and most certainly not lead in wealth creation. The struggle for Africa's economic independence is about using information as a lever for wealth creation.

The other day I was listening to an interview on TV with the creator of the South African TV series 'Generations'. He said when he came up with the idea to start the series he needed information. He ordered a book from America, read it from start to finish and followed it step by step in creating the now famous 'Generations'. Many of us have ideas and we cannot afford to get the best coaches and mentors as we do not have many among our own people. But we can follow the example of the creator of 'Generations'. All the information we need is now available in books, tapes or on the internet. The challenge is whether we have the capacity to see and get the wealth hidden in the information.

Post colonial knowledge and Africa's oral culture

It is knowledge that rules the world and the creators and more importantly users of useful knowledge rule the world economically, politically, technologically and culturally. We need post-colonial knowledge because today Africa is not independent in its knowledge. We have not created our own knowledge and still depend on the knowledge of our colonial masters. The trend of knowledge flow today is still in West-to-Africa fashion and rarely the other way round. If knowledge is the greatest asset in wealth creation, our lack of our own stock of knowledge explains why we are where we are economically. Much of the little writing I see from Africa is fiction and this is the area we get awards for.

We need more non-fiction writing that can help us move forward economically, politically, technologically and culturally and these must be written from a post-colonial perspective in the interest of Africans. One of the greatest needs of Africa today is African authors with ability to communicate non-fiction material to the people in an inspiring and challenging way. This type of writing should also enable us to express ourselves on the world stage. We need to balance the flow of knowledge both ways. This means three things. First, our writing standards must equal the best in the world to get any attention on the crowded market. Besides, our packaging quality must also equal the best in the world. And lastly, we need a lot of work to be done on distribution both within and without the continent. We need to establish partnerships within the continent and with others outside the continent. Our brothers and sisters in the Diaspora can play a major role in this. The greatest challenge however is the quality of our writing, printing and packaging because the best will always sell no matter where it comes from. I get put off to recognize an African book by its inferior quality, printing and packaging. No wonder such books cannot get any serious attention on the international market. We need more high quality economic, political, technological and cultural books on Africa as a whole by African authors.

Our culture is an oral culture. In the knowledge era while this culture has its place, it is a very big liability if it is the only mode we use for our knowledge management. To survive in today's world one has to get the best knowledge in the world on what he or she does through reading the best material in the world available, upgrading through short courses and other means and getting the best mentors and coaches one can afford. If we are serious about the struggle for the economic liberation for Africa we need a significant shift from our oral culture to a reading or documentation culture.

Our authors have the obligation to write the best materials and we have the obligation to read their writings. Africans generally do not read except for news, for examination purposes and report writing at work. We cannot begin to talk about the struggle for the economic liberation of Africa without developing a reading culture. Some people have a way of misunderstanding even the clearest message. By saying we should read the materials or writings or buy African books I do not in any way imply that we should boycott information and knowledge from the West for we cannot. All I am talking about is balancing.

A challenge for our authors is to simplify their writing. When we take our writing to the public the aim is to communicate and not impress. I have a doctorate degree in Development Studies but sometimes I read some articles in a newspaper and I have to struggle to comprehend what the author is saying because of the sophistication of the writing. I often imagine what the situation can be to someone of low education to grasp concepts I grapple with simply because they were written with sophistication to impress rather than to serve. This is one of the problems that put our people off reading and in the course, discourage the reading culture. If we want to impress each other let us do it in our academic fora but when we come to the public domain, let us be as simple as possible and communicate in a language our people will understand. I am told that Albert Einstein employed a communications expert whom he worked with over long periods of time sometimes up to three years to help him bring to the general public some of his scientific theories.

When I write, I give some samples of my writings to my ten-year old daughter to read. Later I ask her to tell me what she has managed to get from the reading. If she struggles to repeat the content, I know that I still have some work to do in revising my writing, to simplify it further. To communicate to the public in a generally low literacy environment, we must target the ten-year mind because the grasp and comprehension ability by most of our people is more or less at that level.

As we shift from oral to reading culture we also need to develop the capacity to differentiate between useful and not so useful information and knowledge. The market is crowded with so much information, inviting our attention. We are experiencing an information overload or saturation but not all of that information is useful in the struggle for economic liberation of Africa. According to Rothwell and Sulivan (2005: 43):

- The amount of information created over the last thirty years is greater than what was produced in the previous five thousand years.
- More than 100, 000 book titles are published in the US alone every year. World wide the number could exceed one million.
- The amount of information stored online now is more than 2.5 times what is found on paper, and human knowledge, at least measured by the amount of information available on-line, is doubling every one hundred years.
- We are all experiencing an invasion of our time with tremendous amount of phone calls, e-mails and voice mails.

The key question is how much of the over-abundant information is created by Africans and can it be useful in the struggle for the economic liberation for Africa? We need to sieve out that information which is useful for the economic liberation of Africa and create new information to fill the gaps. This is why knowledge management is such a key skill in the struggle for the economic liberation for Africa.

Useful information or knowledge is that which will enable the individual to make some economic, political, technological or cultural contribution. In short, it is information or knowledge that can be used in the struggle for the economic liberation of the continent. There is no need to waste time with irrelevant information or knowledge. A local saying substantiates this: *there are so many good things in life but they are not all meant for you.* Let us get only that information that is meant for us and our interests. Useful information must help entrench the fact that Africa is not economically independent and that this is the most formidable challenge facing Africa today. It must facilitate the process of turning resources into wealth. It must facilitate the acquisition of assets and businesses. The information must convince us on the need to patronize businesses owned by Africans and help the owners of the businesses to be easy to do business with.

I see that all over Africa, there is a lot of work to be done in improving the reading culture. I went to a book fair and at that fair there were more books than people! If you go to an average bookshop in Africa there will be more people of other races than the Africans themselves patronizing it.

Conclusion

Africa is poor not because it lacks the resources. It is poor because it has failed to transform its resources into wealth. Wealth comes from trade and not aid. The world has created a system and barriers that are constructed in such a way that Africa may not develop and will continue to be exploited. To break the barriers and become an equal player, Africa will need to identify its niche or its usefulness in the world and invest in knowledge management as a lever for transforming its resources into finished products and services.

In the knowledge economy it is ideas that sell and create wealth. We need to come up with million or billion dollar ideas. We need through creative imagination to clothe the ideas with information in order to turn them into world class products or services. We then need the initiative to boldly take the finished products or services to the world market. I came up with the idea that African proverbs can be used as a more effective tool for improving organizational and institutional performance. I creatively combined the idea with the theory and practice of organization development to create best selling books. I then took the books to the world market. The rest of the story is obvious.

The continent is on a perilous road with a real possibility of sinking into the abyss of oblivion but this world has always been enlightened by ideas. Powerful ideas can overwrite and override the destiny written for us by our own ignorance and manipulations of others. Ideas can bring economic independence. Ideas can make a brand new beginning possible. The hope of the continent is in the emergence of those ideas that can bring economic independence and sanity to the reigning chaos created by capitalism without human values.

One proverb summarizes the argument through a question: *what business does an egg have dancing with the stones?* Africa has been the case of an egg dancing with stones in the intense dance of survival of the fittest. Continued dancing at this party will only lead to oblivion. Africa's hope is only to turn into a stone herself through becoming economically independent.

CHAPTER 4: AFRICAN POLITICS AND ECONOMIC DEVELOPMENT

Introduction

Buckminister Fuller constantly argued that this world can be better off without politicians. He stated that if we took away all the industrial machinery and mechanisms for doing business and leave all political leaders intact, within six months two billion people would die of starvation; go through a lot of pain and deprivation along the way. He also said if the mechanisms for doing business were left intact and the politicians and their organizations were taken away people would keep right on eating and may be getting a little better than before (1969: 157).

Many of the politicians in Africa confirm Professor Fuller's argument. People have generally lost trust in politicians and politics. These have become outdated because the politicians have lost their relevance. They no longer bring any change in people's economic well being except in themselves. To many politicians, politics has become a lucrative business. Elections in many countries have lost meaning. I am afraid to say many of the current presidents on the continent are not the ones people elected. They rigged their way into the office and forced themselves on the people. Because people rejected them, they are not true leaders and it is naïve to expect them to serve the interests of the people. They are in power by their own mandate and not by the mandate of the people. This is a major obstacle to Africa's economic independence – leaders who do not have economic development of their people as their agenda yet holding high positions in the countries, frustrating those few leaders who would want to serve the people.

I remember working in a rural area trying to help the people in a village to create 'visions' of their desired future and that of their village when an old man raised his hand and stopped me. He asked how old I was and before I answered he went on to explain that he had been around during the colonial era, and even during the thirty or so years of the first African president and his party, the ten years of the so called democratically elected president and his party and today with the incumbent president. Then he said during all these periods, nothing had changed in that particular village. If anything the economic situation was deteriorating. He then asked what right or on what basis I was standing on a belief that the future would be different when all the politics of the past had been the same with no sign of change for the future.

Most Africans, like this old man, are fatalistic. Replacing this apathy with a strong 'possibility mentality' is a great leadership challenge on the continent which unfortunately most political and other leaders do not rise up to.

The need for new politics and politicians in Africa

The truth of the matter is that while we may not need most of the politicians, we cannot simply do away with them and the systems they have created. We have to learn to live with them while making efforts to replace them or change the institutions they have created so that they can become agents of economic development. One way of doing this is by ensuring a strong and vibrant civil society as will be discussed in the next chapter. Another way is direct involvement in politics by good people driven by noble intentions to really serve their people as a calling rather than a business. These need to be people who are strong enough not to be changed by the system but to change it. President Barrack Obama's scenario presents a good example of how 'outsiders' can break into the inner circle.

In the 1950s and 60s, the Indian government provided scholarships to promising African students to study in India. The main purpose of the scholarships was not just to offer the qualifications pursued but to give the students space and time to collectively strategize on how to bring about political independence to their countries and the continent as a whole. I strongly believe that today we need a similar initiative whose main purpose would be to help young people to collectively strategize on how to bring about economic independence to their countries and to the continent as a whole. The initiative would be aimed to help them reflect, think and strategize on how to break the aid chain and make the continent stand on her own feet. It would also help them plan and strategize on how to bring about clean and relevant politics on the continent.

I am not a believer of the notion that it took America 200 years and Europe much longer to be where they are today therefore we should be more patient with Africa because after all she is only 50 years old in political independence. I do not believe this because countries like Singapore, Indonesia, South Korea and a few others have shown that it is possible to achieve economic development within one generation. It is not the length of time but the politics and leadership being practiced that matters. President Barrack Obama has shown that if well organized, 'new blood' can oust the 'old guard'. What is needed is vision, a strong conviction, high sense of discipline, strategy and an unstoppable faith for the realization of the vision and execution of the strategy. An initiative aimed at empowering a new political and economic leadership would set Africa on a new and better course towards utopia and away from oblivion where most of the current leaders are taking the continent to.

The need for involvement in the political process
In most African countries, the way people vote in capital cities often represents the true picture of hoped for unbiased results of the presidential, parliamentary and other elections. People in rural areas are often manipulated by misinformation, partisan propaganda, religious and tribal prejudices. The way people vote in capital cities and urban areas in Africa is a good objective way of assessing a country's unbiased opinion of its political preferences. In presidential and parliamentary elections in an African country, if people in rural areas vote significantly differently from those in the capital city or major urban areas, or in short the middle class citizens, and if the people in rural areas vote in favor of the current government when those in the capital city and major urban areas vote overwhelmingly against it, the elections are likely not to have been free and fair. Just as the challenge of economic development in much of Africa is to spread 'development and growth' from capital cities to remote rural areas,

the challenge of political development equally is to spread the way people vote in capital cities to rural areas.

This chapter aims to awaken the consciousness of what I will call 'privileged young adults' based in capital cities and urban areas to their political roles and responsibilities especially in helping people in the rural areas to overcome the various prejudices so that they can vote more independently and take more responsibility of their political destinies. The burden of the chapter is to spread voting patterns in capital cities to remote rural areas. This would contribute greatly towards genuinely free and fair elections. Countries with freer and fairer elections are relatively more politically stable which is a prerequisite for economic and social development. Countries like Botswana, Mozambique and to some extent Tanzania are making progress because of their political stability. Ivory Coast, Sudan, DRC and Zimbabwe, on the other hand, are in socio-economic crises because of political instability as a main cause. Kenya can be added as the most recent case. The significance of political stability is underscored by Kwame Nkrumah who said, *"Seek ye first the political kingdom and all these things (economic and social development) will be added unto thee."* In short, good politics make good economics and bad politics make bad economics.

Privileged young adults and importance of their political involvement

For lack of a better word, by 'privileged young adults' I mean mostly urban based young and successful professional and business people as a group. This group has traditionally been a small section of the African society but currently it is growing very rapidly and provides a rare opportunity in the political development of the continent. The meaning is also extended to include university students and even secondary school students. We could also extend the meaning of privileged young adults to include the individual country and the collective African diaspora. It is very important to note that leaders like Kwame Nkrumah, Nnandi Azikiwe, Jomo Kenyatta, Kamuzu Banda and Kenneth Kaunda started their political activism while in Europe when groups of Africans and Caribbeans used to meet to discuss the political situation back home. Similarly, today's Africans in the diaspora can play a critical role in influencing the political landscape in their countries and the continent as a whole.

Just as many people sleep-walk through life, in much of Africa today, the group we refer to as privileged young adults is still sleeping as far as their political awareness and responsibilities are concerned. They have abdicated this responsibility to politicians (who often do not have the welfare of the people at heart) and ignorant poor rural based masses and the urban poor who often lack organization and objectivity to determine their political preferences and destinies. Many of them have the attitude, *"I have my job and I don't care who wins."* They do not see how politics affect them and their future or that of their children. I was amazed to find out that most of my friends were surprised that I joined the 'Concerned Citizens' to make a contribution towards breaking the budget impasse in parliament described in the next chapter.

Privileged young adults should know that their destiny is tied to that of the poor rural masses and that their 'wise voting' comes to nothing without the cooperation and support and 'wise voting' of the poor rural masses. They should also recognize that *many people smear themselves with mud and then complain that they are dirty.* In other words, they complain about the bad socio-economic situations in their countries forgetting that the pain is self-inflicted through abdication of their political responsibilities and roles especially that of influencing their poor rural and urban counterparts.

Apart from those privileged young adults working directly in political parties and to some extent in human rights NGOs and CSOs, those working in government, business and even the media who happen to be in majority do not see their role in politics at all. This creates a fertile ground for political abuse by selfish political leaders because *where the masses are illiterate, selfish politicians smile.*

Recognizing the crucial role that privileged young adults play in determining a country's political landscape, especially when they wake up to their roles and responsibilities, is crucial for true political independence. Selfish and corrupt political leaders know this no wonder they spend so much time fighting them. This is why Paul Pot of Khmer Rouge in Cambodia exterminated an entire middle class. It is also the same reason Idi Amin fought so ruthlessly against the middle class in Uganda. It is also why up to this day in some African countries we still have informers in the army, the police, the civil service, university faculties and even in communities to act as government machinery to instill fear among the middle class citizens. Such governments spend so much negative energy on their privileged young adults because they know the potential power that these citizens have. *Unless the tree has ripe edible fruits, it is futile to spend time throwing stones into it.*

Civil society efforts aimed at political development and democratization today are rarely consciously targeted at the group I am referring to as privileged young adults. Today this group is a 'forgotten group' among CSOs in their efforts towards democratization and political development of the continent since much of the efforts go towards 'empowering the rural poor masses'. It is important to remember, however, that the force of development in any country is its privileged young adults and no country can rise above its privileged young adults political consciousness as *no stream can rise above its source.* The challenge, therefore, is to fire up the privileged young adults to get concerned and involved enough in influencing, politically and in a positive way, their rural and poor urban counterparts.

Improving political involvement

Nation wide change can be achieved faster if the urban based privileged young adults take political action. More can be achieved in fast tracking political development if the urban based privileged young adults take a more organized and proactive approach in politically influencing the people based in rural areas and those who look up to them as models. They are more strategically positioned to be catalysts of political development because:

- They understand issues and have the capacity to analyze them. They therefore cannot be easily manipulated.
- They can influence grass roots people as they are looked up to as models and through kinships with relatives in rural areas. In much of Africa no one can claim that they come from the city in which they live. Everyone living in the city has a rural home or home of origin in the rural areas. One cannot claim to be truly developed if their home or at least community of origin is not enjoying the 'benefits of development' enjoyed in town. Unless development spreads to the rural areas as well, the development in town remains superficial and not sustainable in the real sense of the word.
- Through electronic and print media, they are easier to mobilize and therefore provide the greatest civil society leverage in empowering rural masses.

Currently however, privileged young adults in Africa are an excluded target group for civil society efforts to democratization and political development. It is important to note that almost all political changes on the continent and elsewhere have been brought about by privileged young adults when they woke up to their political responsibilities. The African founding fathers like Kwame Nkrumah, Jomo Kenyatta, Julius Nyerere, Kamuzu Banda, Kenneth Kaunda and Nelson Mandela are some examples. Martin Luther King Jnr, Malcolm X and Gandhi are other examples further afield. Privileged young adults and not typically poor rural individuals and groups are the ones who have been agents of political change. This is why individuals coming from typically rural areas without the education and resources available to the privileged young adults like Joseph Kony and Alice Lamkwena of Uganda cannot achieve their political goals of becoming national leaders. The best they can achieve is to become guerilla or cult leaders.

The need for the involvement of 'good' people in the political processes of their countries and the continent cannot be overemphasized. Robert Greenleaf (2001: 58 – 59) captures the point well when he argues who the real enemy for good change is through the lengthy quote below:

Who is the enemy? Who is holding back more rapid movement to the better society that is reasonable and possible with available resources? Who is responsible for the mediocre performance of so many of our institutions? Who is standing in the way of a large consensus on the definition of the better society and paths of reaching it?

Not evil people. Not stupid people. Not apathetic people. Not the 'system'. Not the protesters, the disputers, the revolutionaries, the reactionaries.
Granting that fewer evil, stupid, or apathetic people or a better 'system' might make the job easier, their removal would not change matters, not for long. The better society will come, if it comes, with plenty of evil, stupid, apathetic people around and with an imperfect, ponderous, inertia-charged 'system' as vehicle for change. Liquidate the offending people, radically alter or destroy the system, and in less than a generation they will all be back. It is not in the

nature of things that a society can be cleaned up once and for all according to an ideal plan. And even if it were possible, who would want to live in an aseptic world? Evil, stupidity, apathy, the 'system' are not the enemy even though society building forces will be contending with them all the time. The healthy society, like a healthy body, is not one that has taken the most medicine. It is the one in which the internal health building forces are in their best shape.

The real enemy is fuzzy thinking on the part of good, intelligent, vital people, and their failure to lead, and to follow servants as leaders. Too many settle for being critics and experts. There is too much intellectual wheel spinning, too much retreating into 'research'; too little preparation for and willingness to undertake the hard and high risk tasks of building better institutions in an imperfect world, too little disposition to 'the problem' as residing in here and not out there.

In short, the enemy is strong natural servants who have the potential to lead but do not lead, or choose to follow a non-servant leader. They suffer, society suffers. And so it may be in the future.

Taking political responsibility

In bringing up their children, Jews prioritize three issues: education, the need to acquire a survival skill or talent, and political consciousness. This could be one of the reasons why the Jews as a group of people are successful. In Africa, we could do well to follow their example.

Individually each privileged young adult in Africa needs to ask themselves a few introspective and important questions:

- What is my circle of influence as far as politics in my country is concerned?
- How have I or how am I using this circle of influence?
- How can I expand my circle of influence to contribute more to the political development of country and the continent?

Politically conscious parents should take it as their key parental responsibility to teach their children from the earliest age of understanding the meaning of politics and the need to get involved in the political processes of the community and the country. Emphasis should be on what politics is and the differences between positive and negative politics and what to do when one sees negative politics being practiced. Beyond teaching the children through words, the most effective method of teaching them is to let the children see the parents practice what they preach in their every day life – that is to let the children see the parents' own involvement in local and national political processes.

One way to encourage privileged young adults' involvement in politics is to make sure that politics, especially the difference between positive and negative politics, is taught right from kindergarten to secondary school as a compulsory subject. This will greatly help to cultivate proper national values and attitudes towards politics. The emphasis should be: What is politics? How does politics affect us as individuals, families, communities and as a nation? How do we differentiate between negative and positive politics? What should we do when we see negative politics rearing its ugly head?

The church is potentially the most powerful institution in the world as far as molding societal values positively is concerned. While the church may have lost its influence in Europe and other parts of the world, its influence in Africa it is still very strong. Churches and religious institutions, therefore, need to take a key role in teaching their faithfuls, especially the privileged young adults, their rightful roles and responsibilities in politics, especially on how to ensure positive politics and what to do when they see negative politics being practiced. The Pentecostal and charismatic churches which are growing at a very fast rate in most urban areas in Africa have managed to appeal to and capture the privileged young adults as a group. Unfortunately, these and most of the churches do not have 'political conscientization' of their members as one of their key agendas. This is a lost opportunity for them and for their countries and for the continent as a whole. If the church as a whole can put its house in order, refuse to be manipulated by corrupt politicians it can transform the political landscape of the continent within one generation. Unfortunately, some church leadership have come under question for encouraging terrible political systems. History is littered with examples: In Rwanda, some priests participated in the infamous genocide of 1994; in South Africa some churches colluded with the apartheid regime; in the 1960s, Martin Luther King said Sunday 11 a.m. was the most segregated hour in America; and in Malawi, the leadership of Blantyre Synod of the Presbyterian church, the second largest church in the country, supported and preferred section 65 (with the aim to expel some Parliamentarians from Parliament for purely political reasons) to the national budget contrary to the opinion and views of most of its members. Despite these lamentable examples, there is no question that the church can help change the political landscape by focusing its energy on political education of the members and less on fighting each other and other religions.

Civil Society Organizations working in democratization and political development need to deliberately target and prioritize the privileged young adults as a key lever for their efforts. They need to find creative ways of appealing and reaching out to them and getting them engaged in the political processes and development of their countries and the continent. They need to find ways of waking them out of their slumber by showing them the seriousness of the negative consequences of non-involvement. A special group among the privileged young adults in need of such attention is that of popular musicians.

Popular musicians have great influence and appeal to the masses. Many of them, however, are not aware of the enormous power for good they can exert on the masses through carefully crafted messages in their songs. Many of them allow politicians to use them.

In one tour in Uganda while traveling from Jinja to Kampala to see the source of the river Nile, the tour guide treated us to a tape by one of the country's local musician. The entire album was composed of songs in praise of the President and his party and castigating the opposition. The guide told us that the President gave the musician a car, thanking him for the album. I heard a similar song in Malawi by a popular musician, Joseph Nkasa. The title of the song was, *'Today's 'Moses' is Bingu wa Mutharika* (the President)'. Another Malawian musician, Lucias Banda, lost his nationwide reputation as the 'people's musician' after he had allowed himself to be used by former President, Bakili Muluzi for purposes many considered to be selfish.

A recent Reuters report carried the headline: *Senegal bans reggae star for criticizing President.* The article talked about the move by the Senegalese government to ban Ivorian Tiken Jah Fakoly from Senegal after he had made a statement at a show in Dakar asking the President, Abdoulaye Wade, to 'leave power'. There are instances, however, when musicians from elsewhere performed to conscientize the population on progressive politics. Lucky Dube and Bob Marley used their influence to positively contribute to the politics of their countries and the world as a whole. Since popular musicians wield this great influence, there is great need for cooperation between CSOs and popular musicians who may cooperate to work together in political conscientization efforts.

Middle class women as privileged young adults have a big role to change the face of politics too. These need to organize themselves more to form associations with the aim of promoting women involvement in politics. They need to push for more women representation in parliaments, for example. The most important thing they can do after this is to 'apply pressure' on their fellow elected women not to succumb to political party pressures that make them support agendas which are contrary to people's interests. If middle class women organize themselves in this way, they would be a power that cannot be stopped by male selfish politicians.

In short, privileged young adults have three main political roles and responsibilities in leveraging political development processes in their countries and the continent. These are:

- To be involved personally with the aim of shaping the political destinies of their countries in their favor. Involvement must mean going beyond mere words and contributing to phone in programs on radio to organizing themselves for action like taking part in voting and holding politicians accountable to fulfill their promises and imposing sanctions if they fail to fulfill those promises.
- To teach their children the value of being involved in the political processes of their communities and countries.
- To exert influence on the people living in rural areas and poor urban slums who happen to be within their circle of influence.

Conclusion

The hope of cultivating positive politics in Africa lies in having a politically conscious, strong, vibrant privileged young adults that are concerned enough to play their roles and responsibilities. An awakened privileged young adults as a group presents the best opportunity for the consolidation and cultivation of positive politics in Africa. Such a group represents economic, political and spiritual power and influence. The privileged young adults must move beyond complaining about the political situation in their countries and on the continent to taking action. Their greatest contribution would be creating momentum among the rural and urban poor towards getting the right people into elected positions and holding those people accountable. The campaign movement led by Barack Obama to wrestle political power from an established inner circle should teach African youths that they can stand up against dictatorships using 'new methods' for playing the political game.

If one draws the map of Africa, especially sub Saharan Africa, one will notice a high correlation between the socio-economic development of each country and its unified voting patterns between urban and rural areas. This is because *the pot for cooking a lizard and the one for cooking a chameleon must be the same.* We are looking forward to the day in Africa, when voting patterns in capital cities and major urban areas on one hand and the rural areas on the other will be unified and that when the people have spoken the leaders will listen and peacefully leave power to those the people have given the mandate. Privileged young adults have a critical role to play in making this a reality. The importance of getting involved in political development processes and not leaving these to fate is well summarized by the proverb *many people smear themselves with mud and then complain that they are dirty.*

CHAPTER 5: CIVIL SOCIETY AND ECONOMIC DEVELOPMENT

In this chapter I will discuss the contribution civil society organizations can make towards the struggle for Africa's economic independence. In other words, I will argue for the need for civil society organizations to take more interest in economic development efforts and therefore the economic independence of the continent. The base of this argument is the fact that most civil society organizations are focused on social development and they do not consciously take economic development as their main business. But genuine social development can only be built on a strong foundation of economic development. The local economic development observed in Western countries came as a result of an adoption of the private sector as a driving economic force, thus allowing for full integration in the market-led economy (Kyaruzi, 2008; 266). In short, economic development is the basis for economic independence and civil society efforts will be more meaningful if their contribution makes a conscious contribution to economic development in the short and long term

What is civil society?

"Ants united can carry a dead elephant to their cave"

Fowler (2002: 287 – 300) describes civil society as an area for voluntary formal and informal *collective* citizen engagement distinct from families, state and profit-seeking organizations.

Civil society comprises organizations of citizens that come together to pursue interests and purposes for the good of all. They include NGOs, community groups, labor unions, professional associations, faith based organizations and parts of the media and academia. They operate at all levels from grassroots levels at village and community to national and international levels (The Commonwealth Foundation, 2004: 11).

A common mistake is to equate civil society to NGOs. Obviously NGOs are a major player among civil society organizations but they are not the only ones. Of late it is being observed that other players including social movements, social organizations, nationalist and religious groups are gaining ascending prominence in civic engagement with government and other power holders (Nkwachukwu, 2003: 1 – 15; Kaldor, 2003: 12). Social organizations, social movements, religious organizations and various forms of traditional organizations tend to have more social legitimacy than NGOs. They are an expression of the people's own values. They are institutionalized as they form part and parcel of the people's life. The people's attachment and ownership of them is higher. One evidence of this is that people are willing to voluntarily support the institutions' continued existence through their own contributions. Non-governmental organizations, on the other hand, are usually seen as transactional organizations. People expect the NGOs to give them rather than they making contributions to them. They are less attached to the NGOs and they see the NGOs' core business as resource provision rather than a means to express who they are. Most NGOs rarely become entrenched as institutions among the people. When an NGO cuts off resource provision to the people, it almost always loses its relevance among the people it serves. What the foregoing means is that rural people's membership organizations are better able to represent the poor than NGOs and that grassroots organizations are preferable to those induced from outside (Agriculture and Natural Resources Team, 2004: 3). But a key challenge bedeviling these types of organizations in contexts of poverty is lack of capacity due to low political consciousness and lack of economic power. Building capacity for civic engagement with power holders, therefore, must not be limited to NGOs, and NGOs should not monopolize discourses on social accountability.

Fowler (2005: 2) observed that NGOs may be displaced as agents of structural change by member based activist and other civic entities such as religious institutions. For instance, the church played a crucial role and succeeded in thwarting the unconstitutional third term campaign by the former president in Malawi, strengthening the argument that the church or religious institutions may be the most powerful civil society expression in Africa. Although many African presidents have managed to break the spirit and dreams of their people, none has ever succeeded in breaking the church (Lamb, 1987: 143).

The foregoing, however, does not mean that the church in Africa always plays an active civic role. This has been demonstrated by a recent study by Dorman (2002: 75 – 92) on relations between the church and state in Zimbabwe. The study revealed that although the church may play a critical role in opening up space for debate, the state may still co-opt and weaken churches in its effort to retain hegemony.

What is the contribution of civil society?
Civil Society organizations contribute to development in many ways. According to the Commonwealth Foundation (2004: 11), they can:

- raise awareness and understanding of development policies, laws and regulatory institutions.
- provide opportunities for stakeholders to communicate with governance institutions and elected representatives. In particular, civil society organizations can help give voice to marginalized groups.
- provide enriching input into discussions about development policy and implementation strategies. They can suggest and advocate for new perspectives, policies and methodologies.
- make citizens more aware of what social and economic development decisions are being taken, by whom and from what options, on what grounds with what expected results and with what resources to support implementation.
- can play a crucial 'watchdog' role in monitoring the implementation and effects of national and international programs and policies. By increasing public accountability in this way, civil society organizations are promoting both democracy and development.

Civil society organizations and economic development

Civil society organizations can play a more significant role in economic development of the continent. Weak and fragile states as many of them are in Africa require strong civil society organizations in order to progress. Pratt (2008) suggests that in order to be more helpful and fulfill their role, civil society functions can be summarized as: helping generating the social basis for democracy, promoting accountability beyond party politics, producing social trust, reciprocity and collective action; and supporting the rights of citizens and the concept of citizenship.

I would like to add that in all these, civil society organizations must not lose sight of the fact that the real challenge of the continent today is its struggle for economic independence. In the busyness of the activities, this tends to be forgotten leading to priorities that will not help achieve this end. If we are serious about development and economic independence, Africa needs a world where there is a balance of power that makes it possible for small countries to survive and make progress and not to be conquered or absorbed by the rich and powerful countries.

In a paper presented by Kumi Naidoo of Civicus at a recent conference on the role of civil society in the Netherlands, he explained that societal change happens at three levels. These are the *macro*, *meso* and *micro* levels. The macro level refers to the structural world order which is currently designed to serve the interests of the rich and powerful and exclude the poor at a global level. The meso level represents the policy level at national level. The policies too are usually designed to serve the powerful and exclude the poor. In most cases the written policies may be good and well intended but their implementation often does not match up with the original intentions. The *micro* level refers to direct delivery of services in the communities.

The time span to bring about change at these levels is different. It takes about one to five years to bring about change at the *micro* level. It takes about three to ten years to bring about change at the *meso* level. It also takes about ten to twenty years to bring about change at the macro level. It should be noted, however, that change at the lower levels can only be sustainable depending on change at the higher levels. Change at the micro level will therefore be soon eroded if there is no change at the meso and the macro levels. This is a very common story in development work. We know of projects that were very successful and 'star performers' in the 1960s and 70s that today no one remembers. These projects were successful at the micro level with no corresponding change at the meso and macro levels.

As a consultant I am often called and asked to do impact assessments of projects. Many of the development organizations will run five-year projects at community level, often in service delivery. They will call a consultant to do an impact assessment at the closure of the project. But my argument has always been you cannot measure impact soon after the end of the project because whatever force is driving the benefits of the project at this time is the presence of the donor money. The continuity of the benefits after the project has stopped is the true measure of impact and must be given a test of time. For how long will the benefits continue to flow? That is the real measure of impact. The continued flow of the benefits of the project will depend to a great deal on the changes achieved at the meso and macro levels. Measuring impact at the closure of the project therefore makes no sense because at this time there is no way of objectively knowing whether the policy or governance levels have been changed enough to guarantee sustainability of the gains made at the micro level. A true impact assessment in my opinion can only be made at least five years after the closure of the project.

This brings to the question – What should civil society organizations really focus on so that they should make a major contribution towards the economic independence of the continent? According to Naidoo, currently, civil society organizations focus 80 percent of their effort in providing basic services, 15 percent in policy advocacy work and 5 percent in trying to change the global world order or global governance work. The quickest way to achieve economic independence for the continent is to turn the pyramid upside down. If the world order or global governance structures are changed much of the national policies and basic needs of the people in the communities will take care of themselves without needing any intervention of the civil society organizations. This is because the economic development of the world is not a lack of resources but a lack of effective systems that ensure that there is justice and fairness in accessing the resources available especially to the poor people. The struggle for the economic development of the continent is currently being focused on wrong priorities – providing basic services to communities. To bring about real change there is need for refocusing. Bringing the poorest people into the market economy is the central feature of this refocusing.

The current temptation and practice to push civil society organizations to do more service delivery work arises from the donors' need for more visible results within a short time. This is what brings suspicion. It is now common knowledge that service delivery alone is like mending broken chairs on a sinking titanic – why do we still insist on such efforts when we know that they will not bring the results we want? The real work of civil society organizations is to challenge power relations and not to provide services. The current reversal of the functions and role of civil society organizations is a major side track not helping Africa move towards utopia.

The need for international civil society

Moving from service delivery to changing world governance and world order implies the need for collective action beyond the borders. The same applies to very complicated domestic situations like the one in Zimbabwe. If the government of Zimbabwe for example could refuse to give visas to Kofi Annan, Jimmy Carter and Graca Machel, it shows how determined they are to completely shut up civil society voice. It also shows how little if any space the people in that country have to exercise their civic rights. This calls for international civil society intervention because action from within cannot be effective. I know that there were some initiatives in Europe but my feel is that their 'volume of voice' did not match the noise coming from Harare. The only distinct civil society voices so far were those of the Anglican Bishops Desmond Tutu and Sentammu, the bishop of York in the UK who tore his dog collar and vowed never to wear it again until Mugabe has been removed from power by force if necessary.

I would want to point out that the general weakness of civil society in Africa reflects a similar weakness of civil society in Western countries. Civil society organizations in Western countries are failing to confront their government on the negative policies that exclude poor countries from achieving economic independence. The fact that they continue to support their southern counterparts with 80 percent funding towards service delivery when they know pretty well that the challenge of Africa's economic independence does not lie there is their confession of their failure in this regard.

I have been following the main discourses on what to do to help Africa but in all those discourses what I have not heard is a clear discussion on how to help Africa become economically independent by a specific date. This issue is consciously or unconsciously skirted. This is expected because independence is never given. It is demanded and often fought for. It is taken by those demanding it. Independence given on a silver platter is not true independence. The struggle that Gandhi, Martin Luther King Jr, Malcom X, Nelson Mandela were involved in and gave their lives to is far from over. Now it has taken another form, away from political independence to economic independence and the civil society is yet to rise to this challenge and face it squarely. Ironically this is the direction Martin Luther King Jr took through what he called the 'Poor People's Movement' which did not pick up because he was stopped by death.

Where these leaders stopped is where we need to start from. The problem is not business or the market per se but a badly corrupted global economic system that is gyrating far beyond human control leading to more and more people ending in starvation and violence, becoming homeless beggars, welfare recipients or residents of refugee camps (Korten, 1995:13). The majority of these people are in Africa. Raising the floor and bringing these people into the global market economy is the way to balance and reverse the trend. It is a paradox that the global market economy is both a major problem and solution to the economic independence of the continent.

Civil society represents a great force for economic independence but currently much of its energy is misdirected. In fighting for Africa's economic independence, the civil society organizations are fighting in the wrong battle ground – in the communities, funding and supporting service delivery. The real enemy and therefore the real battle ground is in the global governance structures. That is where the struggle for Africa's economic independence must be fought tooth and nail. That is where the war will be lost or won. That is where Gandhi, Martin Luther King, Malcom X, Mandela and Barrack Obama fought and that is why they won. We do not hear much about their counterparts who were trying to solve the problems by concentrating on basic service delivery to people in communities. Alan Fowler and Michael Edwards (2002: 8) rightly observe when they write, "What will make a difference to global poverty in the years to come will not be the number of villages that are served or children that are sponsored, but how grassroots action is connected to the markets and politics at multiple levels of the world system, a collective task in which the ability of the NGOs to work together will be critical." Castro (2007: 386) captures the point well when he observes,

> There is no capitalism today. There is no competition. Today what we have are monopolies in all the great sectors. There is some competition between certain countries to produce television or computers but capitalism does not exist anymore.
>
> Five hundred global corporations today control 80% of the world's economy. Prices don't stem from competition. The price at which, for example medicine to fight AIDS is sold is monopolized. Medicine continues to be one of the most abusive extravagant and exploitative items in the world's budgets...Advertising practically determines who sells and who doesn't. The person who does not have much money cannot advertise his products in any way, even if they are excellent.
>
> After the last world wide bloodbath in the forties, we were promised a world of peace, we were promised that the gap between the rich and the poor would be closed and that the more developed would help the less developed. All this was a huge lie. A world order was imposed on us that cannot be justified, cannot be sustained and cannot be borne. The world is being driven into a dead end street".

Restriction of access to the markets of rich countries at fair terms is a major barrier to trade and economic development among African countries. Tariff barriers can be as high as four times to those paid by developed countries. The barriers according to some estimates cost poor countries $100 billion (Wikipedia, 2008) a year twice as much as they receive in aid. In addition to the tariffs, rich countries and regions like the US and EU limit poor countries' access to their markets. The generous subsidies that rich countries give to their farmers make it difficult for poor farmers in poor countries to compete with them. Over-production from EU's agricultural subsidies encourages overproduction of such goods as tomatoes or sugar which in turn are sold cheaply or dumped to poor countries. Local farmers cannot sell their goods as cheaply and they are moved out of business.

The contradiction of Western countries in their trade practices which are aimed at maintaining an economic world order are further well captured by the Chinese minister of commerce in the BBC interview in 2005 when he said,

> I think the doctrine of free trade is an outstanding one. The free trade doctrine has propelled the economies of Europe and the US to a soaring path of development over the last 200 years. It has also been a doctrine that Europe and America have propagated as glorious doctrine. They have brandished the banner of free trade and gone around the world doing commerce and making money, and becoming developed countries. But now that a developing country that is quite poor and has a GDP per capita of only one thirtieth of theirs has found a few textile companies that can finally compete with European

counterparts, they want to close their doors and engage in protectionism. This, in fact, is a double standard. When they had a comparative advantage, they encouraged the whole world to open their doors, but when they discover that one developing country is becoming more competitive, they say, 'OK, enough. Let's close the door now (Kynge, 2006: 117, 118).

Although China and India are rising to balance world powers, the controlling organizations remain in the hands of the West. Whether it is the futures trade in oil, or commodities exchanges setting the terms of trade for raw materials of goods, the authorities remain largely in the hands of the West leading to adverse trade terms, high costs of commercial transactions and difficulties in accessing products and services (Bawnegie, 2008: 7).

Professor Jeffrey Sachs argues that the work of international civil society would make more impact if they focused on the behavior of rich governments, especially the United States to honor their commitments to help the poor move from poverty and to honor their commitments to limit environmental degradation, climate change and loss of biodiversity. He also urges international civil society to fight for more investment by the large companies in poorest countries. He says the World Trade Organization needs to follow through the political commitments made at Doha and elsewhere to ensure that the poorest countries have access to the markets of the richest (Sachs, 2005: 358, 359). According to Kumi Naidoo, this is where 80 percent of civil society effort should go.

I believe that 50 percent of the African problem has its root causes in Africa mostly due to the failure of the continent to consciously take responsibility for the continent's economic destiny. I believe the other 50 percent is exogenous to Africa. It is in the world order discussed above. Former South African president rightly observed when he said, "The second millennium provided humanity with capital, and technology and the human skills to end poverty and underdevelopment throughout the world but we have refused to use this enormous capacity to end the contemporary, deliberate and savage violence of poverty and underdevelopment" (Mbeki, 2001: 14). Fighting for economic independence, therefore, will mean rising up to the challenge of taking responsibility for the continent's economic destiny and in organizing and mobilizing civil society for structural change in the world order which is currently designed to keep Africa in economic destitution for ever.

This is the magnitude of the challenge that civil society organizations have to rise up to. Unfortunately, this is not the type of language civil society organizations have began to learn and speak. Anything short of attempts to at least influence the world order is merely treating symptoms leaving the root cause intact. *If you cut a piece of a liana creeper without removing the roots it will continue to creep.*

The role of religion in civil society efforts

Religion is now being increasingly recognized as having great potential to contribute towards development. The center of gravity of organized religion, especially Christianity has shifted to Africa. But what is the role of religion in development? Currently, much of its role is in providing services through faith based organizations. Among the stated advantages of the faith based organizations are that: they are values-based which I am not sure whether they mean their staff are motivated by values or that they try to impart 'good' values to the people they work with, they have a wider geographical reach and can easily connect with the people they serve. While this is very important and indeed the different religions are playing an increasingly important role in this matter, my own conviction is that religion in general, in addition to 'projects' through their faith based organizations, need to seriously think through what their truly unique contribution to the economic independence of the continent can be. What is it that only religions can do and no secular organization can do that contributes towards swifter speed to the continent's economic independence? What is the distinct voice of religion in this matter? This is a question I do not hear much debate on.

For me the issue is what difference does religion make in the lives of their members in relation to those members sense of responsibility of the economic independence of the continent. For me a unique contribution of the religions would come from the pulpit. It would be about the cultivation of (spiritual) values that the faithfuls can demonstrate in their practical lives – values that give them a sense of responsibility beyond self to their community's, country's and the continent's economic independence. This is because development is so not much about our *doing* but our *being* and I cannot think of any other institution better placed than religion in cultivating the people's *being*.

The role of religion is not to provide services only nor to challenge powers that be but also and primarily: the cultivation of spiritual values the practice of which can change the way people conduct their lives and business. This is the core business of religion. This is what they can do better than anyone else. Unfortunately, this is not being given the attention it deserves. Norman (1979: 11) observed that, "Christianity today eschews traditional doctrinal priorities and is about its applications. The church is increasingly preoccupied with a more just society and with the material problems of humanity'. My argument is, in trying to bring about a more just society and addressing the material problems of humanity the church or religion's lever is their focus on cultivating spiritual values of their members that the members can practically live out in the way they conduct their lives and their businesses. They should not lose sight of this uniqueness. The loss of this uniqueness is what has largely led to the demise of organized religion in many of the Western countries.

Mobilizing citizens to claim their rights

Changing power relations involves mobilizing people and empowering them to demand their rights. The common practice among civil society organizations in Africa is the CSOs themselves speaking on behalf of the people but not the people speaking for themselves. I remember a social movement I was personally involved in that showed the importance of letting people speak for themselves rather than speaking on their behalf. I was going to attend an annual general meeting of one of my client organizations when I was diverted to an adjacent room where a separate meeting was going on. When I entered the room I was surprised at the composition of the participants and the issue they were discussing. There were young businessmen and women, teachers, lawyers, economists, students, chief executives, traditional leaders and many others. They were discussing how to force Parliament to put aside its political fights and concentrate on meeting the people's expectations. At this particular time, we had a situation in Malawi in which the government was in a minority (with fewer MPs in parliament than those on the opposition side). The opposition, therefore, used to occasionally flex its muscles by using its numerical advantage in the parliament.

To give some brief background to the meeting referred to above, Malawi adopted a multiparty system of government in 1994 when people voted out the then ruling party which had operated as the sole party with the same president since independence in 1964. The new constitution, which was adopted after the new government came in (in 1994), states that a ruling president can rule for a maximum of two consecutive five-year terms. Not so surprisingly, as is still common in Africa, after his two consecutive terms, the president wanted to change the constitution to allow for a third term or even an open term for the incumbent president. People successfully rejected that idea and therefore he was effectively blocked from contesting for the presidency for the third time. Desperate not to lose power, the president handpicked a less known individual from outside his party, apparently he could not trust his party members, and made him the presidential candidate with the understanding that the new president would play by his rules. They campaigned heavily and tirelessly and the candidate won the presidential elections though not without controversy. He won with 31 percent of the votes and many people believed the elections were rigged.

It is rumored that the former president wrote the acceptance speech for the new president (the inauguration ceremony took place before the counting of the votes was completed – not an uncommon practice in Africa). It is also rumored the new president put aside the former president's speech and gave his own which set a clear and different agenda from the party and policies of the former president. This was the beginning of the divergence between the two individuals. Within a short time, the differences became so sharp that they could not continue being in the same party. The new president moved out of the party and formed his own party. A few MPs followed him. This made the party that got him into power become an opposition party while his party that never existed before the elections became the ruling party. The 'new' opposition party joined with other opposition parties in parliament to 'avenge' the betrayal.

The bitterness and anger from the fallout therefore was mostly displayed through frustrating the government agenda in parliament through refusing to pass obviously beneficial bills and through the 'policy of no-cooperation'. One particular point that the former president and his MPs capitalized on was a section in the constitution which stated that if a member of parliament 'crosses the floor' or defects to another party (away from the one that elected him or her to parliament), then that member of parliament forfeits his or her parliamentary seat. They would need to go back to their constituents to seek a fresh mandate through another election. This section had been constantly violated during the former president's regime but it was never invoked because some people felt it was in contradiction with another section of the constitution that provides for freedom of association even to join or withdraw from political parties for everyone including members of parliament.

In order to 'hit back' the former MPs of the former president demanded that this section be invoked which effectively meant that most of the government MPs who were already in minority would be wiped out. The 'ruling party' insisted that the real motive of the opposition party was not to uphold the spirit of constitutionalism but to remove the ruling party MPs with the sinister motive to proceed to impeach the president on flimsy grounds as there would be no MPs to defend him in the parliament.

The opposition members of parliament threatened that they would not vote for the passing of the national budget if the section on crossing the floor was not invoked first. The 'ruling party' said they were not going to agree to have the section invoked when they were sure what the true motives of the opposition MPs were. Since the opposition MPs were in majority the budget was not going to be passed either. Each side took a strong stand and this created an impasse.

It was very clear that for the first time in the history of the country, there was going to be no national budget. There was going to be no national budget not because there was no money but because of political games. For the first time people became consciously aware of the importance of a national budget and what its absence would mean. The meeting I went to was discussing this agenda and what action to take to force Parliament to pass the national budget. The people called themselves 'concerned citizens'. They represented the general society and the concerns of the different categories of people in the society. Their concern was that parliament is supposed to serve the people and not to play games at the expense of the people's lives. From a series of meetings they came up with a strategy the goal of which was to mount pressure on the MPs to pass the budget forthwith. The strategy was launched at a mass rally that drew a crowd of one hundred thousand people (quite a large number in the Malawian context). The strategy included an eight point plan involving:

- Asking the president to call for an immediate reconvening of Parliament (it had been closed because the MPs could not agree on the agenda) to discuss and pass the budget within a specified number of days
- Personal meetings with the president and leaders of opposition parties represented in parliament to lobby with them to resolve their differences and let the budget be passed

If the above measures failed, then ask the citizens to:

- Cut the electricity supply to the MPs homes as this is a public service requiring the national budget.
- Block the MPs from using the public roads.
- Cut off the water supply to the MPs homes.
- Not allow their children to attend public schools.
- Not allow the MPs access airports to get out of the country to get services which they were denying the citizens to get by refusing to pass the budget.
- Effect a 'citizen arrest' on the MPs.

These would be implemented they said, incrementally, corresponding to the resistance from the MPs. To cut a long story short, the MPs became so frightened and quickly passed the budget. They had never faced such an avalanche of pressure from the public which is often assumed very docile. The concerned citizens, indeed, all the citizens did not need to implement all or even many of their action points.

Civil society success factors

A number of lessons can be drawn from the above case which can help point out to some critical success factors for civil society organizations in general. These include:

Relevance – The real driving force was the significance and relevance of the issue at hand. Everyone saw the economic implications of not having the budget passed and what would happen if the people did not act. People can only be mobilized in large numbers on issues that have a direct implication on them. In Africa, issues with direct implication on the people's lives refer to their economic welfare. All the causes that need to draw large enough numbers of people must be communicated in economic terms. This is the language people will understand.

Leadership and its legitimacy – Legitimacy means connecting with people at a deep, values and emotional levels, to ensure real ownership of the issue at hand among them. People can only be moved when they are touched at the emotional level. The ability to touch people at the emotional and values levels calls for great and effective leadership. The 'concerned citizens' represented this type of leadership. They represented a new type of leadership. These were people that the nation had not seen before. They had not even been heard about before. It was a leadership that emerged in response to a situation. It was a clean leadership that reflected the people's values – a direct contrast to much of the conventional leadership that most people had lost trust in. By representing the values of the people, this leadership was able to connect with the people at values level.

Africa today desperately needs new leaders. We need 'new blood' in leadership. Most of the leaders we have are the same ones we had in the 1960s. They just recycle within the inner circle. It is very difficult for young and ambitious people to break into the inner circle because the old guard does not give space. There is nothing wrong continuing being a leader over such a long period of time. The real worry is that most of those leaders have not shifted to

21st century thinking and leadership styles thereby keeping their countries stuck in the past rather than moving into the future. Africa needs leaders who are selfless, can be trusted, can give people confidence that it is possible to bring about change, create a vision of a desired future, a frightening enough picture of what might happen if people do not take action. Africa needs leaders who can stick to a limited number of ideas and communicate them effectively from as many angles as possible until they are internalized in the people's collective subconscious. And one such idea is the idea of Africa's economic independence. At the present stage of development of Africa it is almost a sin for an individual to take or accept a key leadership position if they know they have no capacity to make a contribution directly or indirectly towards the economic independence of the continent.

Transcending 'NGOization' – civil society organizations have mostly been equated to NGOs. But to bring about real change, civil society organizations must be understood to mean much more than just NGOs. In the case above, the avalanche of pressure put on the MPs came from all sorts of groups of people and organizations. This included NGOs, churches, music bands, different types of professional associations, business people, students, traditional groups just to mention a few. The challenges faced are so great that no single group or organization can solve them alone. This also calls for the need to think beyond national borders. Challenges in countries like Zimbabwe where the civil society voice was completely silenced can only benefit from civil society from outside the borders. International civil society has an obligation to bring pressure on relevant bodies that have power to bring about solution to situations like that in Zimbabwe.

Related to the foregoing, part of the success of the campaign was to transcend the current modes of funding NGOs which serve donors' interests more than the interests of the people being helped. The concerned citizens campaign was successful because international NGOs and donors went out of their usual rigid ways of funding and funded the campaign very flexibly. They were able to bear the complexity and uncertainty of the process which is no different from all other development work no matter the nature. They were able to give up the usual control they want to have over the results from the money they give. In addition, the funding by the donors formed only a very small percentage of the total funds of the campaign. A major portion of the funds came from the poor people's own small contributions to the campaign's bank account and at the mass rally. The business people and the different professional associations made generous contributions.

It is important to note the key role students played in the campaign. University students, because of the special role of the institution of the university in society, represent a special force for change. They are looked up to as models by other youths. Their parents respect them and listen to them. They cannot be easily manipulated and they make intelligent arguments. Most importantly they have the energy and confidence based on their status and can intimidate any negative force. University students ought to be given more space in civil society efforts.

Leveraging technology played a key role in the concerned citizens' movement. Driven by the university students and other young professionals, the country was easily ignited to a collective action using the internet and the cell phone. This made simultaneous nationwide communication and coordination possible in such a way that baffled the MPs. The whole country was able to move as one group because of the way technology was leveraged. IC technologies provide a real opportunity but as in many countries in Africa the state monopolizes the TV, the radio and newspapers. Leveraging the internet and the cellphone provides a way to go around this hurdle.

Conclusion

As far as economic independence of the continent is concerned there is an urgent need for national and continent-wide 'economic independence movement' whose explicit goal is to bring about economic liberation for the countries and the continent as a whole. The movement will require a new form of leadership from what we have experienced so far; it will need to transcend the current 'NGOization'; and it will need to leverage technology to build national continental momentum. It will also need 'space to operate' provided by the respective governments and donors genuinely interested in the continent's economic independence.

For a long time, we in Africa have been under the impression that people in Europe and America know better how to solve our problems. But 50 years of their help and 'better knowledge' has proved to the contrary. We have been walking in the crutches of aid instead of walking with our own feet. We have been looking for solutions from outside instead of looking for the solution within ourselves. The leadership provided by the above suggested 'economic independence movement' would provide the leadership we need to focus our new attention to. The power of civil society is in the collective action of its numerous players. The proverbs – *when cobwebs unite, they can tie up a lion* and *ants united can carry a dead elephant to their cave* dramatize this point well.

CHAPTER 6: AFRICAN CULTURE AND ECONOMIC DEVELOPMENT

Introduction

The role of culture in economic development has mostly been ignored. According to Goussikindey (2007: 3) most discussions on Africa's economic development, the facts usually mentioned include:

- Half of Africa's 800 million people live on less than a dollar a day
- Around 80% of the HIV positive population of the world lives in Africa
- Life expectancy on the continent is below 55 years and is rapidly declining in many countries while the birth rates are increasing
- Out of its 54 nations, 34 rank among the world's poorest countries
- Africa accounts for a mere 2 percent of world exports and the wealth generated corresponds to a mere 1.3 percent of the world GDP
- Africa receives 1 percent of the world's total private investment; and
- Despite an estimated $350 billion sunk into Africa in development aid over the past 50 years, million of Africans are now poorer than they were in the 1960s.

As one can observe, in the list above, the issue of culture and its role in economic development is not mentioned. The same is also observed in the most cited suggested solutions to Africa's economic arrest. The solutions typically include:

- Work on comprehensive debt relief
- Combat corruption
- Promote human rights and democracy
- Promote good governance and accountability
- Increase aid and freer trade with the world market and within Africa
- Put an end to wars and ethnic conflicts

Even in the proposed solutions one observes that conscious cultural modification or transformation is not mentioned. This is despite the fact that culture does function both as a 'force of inertia' resisting any change as well as a springboard that can set in motion with intensity any new beginning including economic development.

Culture is not static; it is dynamic. Culture is a continuous process of change but in spite of the change, culture continues giving a community a sense of identity, dignity, continuity, security and binds society together (Muyale-Manenji, 1998: 1). Culture determines a people's values. These values may be supportive or detrimental to economic development. Poverty is not a divine order. It is mostly man-made and there is no lack of knowledge on how to eliminate it. The real challenge is cultural and values based. Others have gone so far as to claim that economic development is not primarily an economic problem but a cultural one (Rahnema and Bawtree, 1997: 30).

While it is not fair or realistic to generalize about the whole continent's culture just as it is not realistic to generalize about cultures of America, Europe or Asia, there are distinct characteristics of the African culture that differentiate it from the other people groups. In much of sub-Saharan Africa, the main characteristic of the culture is its people centeredness now commonly referred to as *ubuntu* by the Bantu people of East and Southern Africa. Ubuntu means *I am because you are and you are because I am* (Mapadimeng, 2007: 258) or humans are humans because of other humans. This chapter will explore how the practice of ubuntu on the continent is both a problem and solution to Africa's economic arrest.

The issue is not romanticizing a historical culture but rediscovering those elements of the culture that have relevance today and can be used as an economic springboard while abandoning those that have become impediments to economic development. It is also about adopting positive elements from other cultures that can help positively in achieving the goal of economic development. The key questions about culture and its relationship with economic development therefore are:

- How congruent are the people's cultural values with economic development?
- Which ones need to be maintained and supported?
- Which ones need to be discarded because they are an impediment to economic development?
- Which ones need to be modified?

Ubuntu: the culture of African people

A people's culture is recognized and taken seriously in this world as a result of that people's achievement in some aspect of life like economy, technology and politics. Now we talk of the Chinese culture, the Japanese culture and the Indian culture because of those particular peoples' achievements. Perceived failing groups tend to abandon their cultures in favor of those cultures perceived to be more successful (this is especially true among the young people). This is an explanation of the onslaught of Western culture on the African continent. African culture was undermined by the processes of colonization, de-culturalization and de-spiritualization. This led to the belief by many Africans that in order to become like the 'successful' West they had to adopt the culture of the West (Maathai, 1995: 18). The Japanese model of economic development is sharply divergent from the Western model in the sense that it is based upon the ancient Confucian and native Japanese traditions of harmony, self-sacrifice and non-individualistic group striving in pursuit of a common cause. The Singaporean economic miracle was based on the values of social cohesion through sharing the benefits of progress, equal opportunities for all, and meritocracy, with the best men and women for the job, especially as leaders of government; and a savings and investment culture (Lee Kuan Yew, 2000: 691). These are similar values to African values but the difference is that the Japanese have consciously integrated these into their economic development and independence efforts.

In Africa the values are disconnected from the 'modern life' creating a gap that is filled largely with Western values of immediate gratification and individualism, for example. And since Africa has not started her march towards economic independence for real the role of values and culture in achieving economic independence in general is unconscious. A rediscovery of ubuntu, its positive attributes and how to employ them in economic development is a major challenge on the continent. Ubuntu – the essence of being human – is built on the five principles of:

- Sharing and collective ownership of opportunities, responsibilities and challenges
- The importance of people and relationships over things
- Participatory decision making and leadership
- Patriotism or loyalty; and
- Reconciliation as a goal of conflict management.

In traditional Africa, these principles were practiced in a generally stable and predictable environment. The challenge facing ubuntu today is that it has generally failed to change with time and transcend the stable and predictable context to ensure continued global relevance. This has resulted in certain shadows being cast over the current practice of ubuntu especially as it has to do with economic empowerment of the African people (Malunga, 2004: 11). Some of these shadows include: massive migration to other continents, inability to correct things when they go wrong or inability to confront issues or give each other constructive negative feedback, mediocrity, immediate gratification tendencies, lack of patriotism, wasteful practices and wholesale adoption of other peoples' values. For a full discussion on the applicability of the positive elements of ubuntu in modern society see my paper: Learning Leadership Development from African Cultures published as INTRAC Praxis note 25 at www.intrac.org

Migration

Africa has more of its professionals working outside the continent than those working on the continent. It is said that the city of Manchester alone in the U.K has more Malawian doctors than all the doctors in Malawi for example (Naidoo, 2007). The rate at which the professionals are leaving the continent is increasing at an alarming rate. Approximately 70,000 skilled graduates leave the continent every year (Calderisi, 2007: 5). In fact, it is not only professionals who migrate. A larger number is that of illegal and non professional immigrants. In fact, in most countries on the continent those who can migrate will migrate. A continent that is continually drained of its human capital cannot develop.

It is understood that people will migrate for a better life as there are less opportunities back home. It is also believed that migration makes economic sense as those who have migrated can support their families back home through remittances. In fact during the years 2000 – 2003 remittances from Africans working abroad averaged $ 17 billion per annum overtaking Foreign Direct Investment flows which averaged $ 15 billion during the same period (UN, 2005). Remittances play a critical economic and financial role as they reach households more directly and augment their resources, reduce consumption gaps, provide working capital and have a multiplier effect through the household's spending within their community.

Although remittances have generally been increasing, Africa receives just 4 percent of the total remittances – by far the smallest share to the developing countries. Among the top 25 recipients only Nigeria was in Africa (Gupta, Pattilo and Wagh, 2007). Given the numbers of people migrating from the continent annually, this means the culture of sending remittances back home is not strong among the Africans. It may also mean that those who fail to find proper jobs cannot afford to send remittances back home. Mohamoud (2007: 197) observes that African diasporas lack the capacity to make their activities more visible to the wider public; their social organization is weak and remain informal; they lack channels to gain access to useful information and networks; and compared with other migrant groups, African associations are linked marginally with the mainstream development agencies.

The key issue for migrants is – *the river that forgets its source will soon dry up* – do they still remember home and the economic welfare of their countries and the continent?

Another issue is where they are most needed or where they would make the most difference. It makes sense for those who hold professional and technical jobs corresponding with their qualifications and experience but it is incomprehensible for people with higher degrees – masters, PhDs to be doing menial jobs just for the sake of staying in Europe or America when they know pretty well that they would be much more useful back home. Before migrating, young people especially the professionals need to seriously consider the pros and cons of their decision in regard to the economic struggle for their countries and for the continent.

One key consideration against emigration is that if one can achieve success on the continent they can become a much more effective role model to others by demonstrating that it is possible to make it even here at home. In the globalized world, a challenge and opportunity is to think of ways to make the same amount of money one could make in Europe or America without having to leave the continent. Through networks and strategic alliances with individuals and institutions in the West, for example, it is possible to find ways of creating value to them that can attract their capital to us right here on the continent.

Migrant Africans have a responsibility to make sure that individually and collectively their contribution to their families, nations and the continent is better than if they had not migrated. If this is not the case, then their migration is in vain as far as the economic development of their countries and the continent is concerned. They would have been much better off back home. Remittances on the other hand cannot substitute for a sustained, domestically driven development effort. Large scale migration hurts domestic labor supply especially if those migrating are highly qualified personnel like is the case in Africa.

Not speaking out when things go wrong

The second demon is inability to correct each other when things go wrong. I was watching CNN soon after the controversial Zimbabwe run-off elections. Former President George Bush speaking on behalf of the G8, spoke strongly and condemned Mugabe. Standing by his side, President Jakaya Kikwete of Tanzania in response to George Bush simply said, 'As Africans we see the situation in Zimbabwe differently' and didn't in anyway condemn Mugabe. Except for Botswana and Zambia and the Prime Minister of Kenya, Raila Odinga, no African country condemned Mugabe. No individual African leaders except for Bishop Desmond Tutu openly condemned Mugabe or asked him to step down. Mugabe is hero in African Union or how else can we explain the silence of the African Union leaders? The suffering and the economic crisis in Zimbabwe and the complication that will be created by the continued presence of Mugabe as a leader of that country deserved the strongest condemnation from leaders of the continent. Of course, it is understood that to point a finger of blame one must stand on a higher moral ground. The failure by our leaders to speak against what is clearly wrong like the elections in Zimbabwe and Kenya leaves a lot to be desired.

Not speaking out when things go wrong or holding each other accountable is also observed in African leaders' failure to adopt NEPAD's agreement for policing each other's progress towards more accountability, democracy and respect for human rights. Despite the West's promise to help this initiative, African leaders have generally failed to live up to these agreements (Meredith, 2006: 679). Obvious mistakes are usually excused in the name of 'our young democracy' or 'this is the African way of doing things and we do not want interference from the West' and 'we are sovereign states therefore we decide what we do even if it is wrong, we have a right to make mistakes'. But the question is at whose expense are those mistakes? The admonition from Nelson Mandela addressing an OAU meeting in 1994 rings more true each passing day: "We must face the matter squarely that where there is something wrong in how we govern ourselves, it must be said that the fault is not in our stars but in ourselves that we are ill governed" (Meredith, 2006: 675).

Culture of mediocrity

Mediocrity is another shadow undermining Africa's economic progress. The failure to put in place standards and enforce them is a clear example. In many African countries there are no clear and enforceable standards on schools and hospitals, for example. There are no standards for roads and this does not seem to bother anyone at all. In fact some of the African leaders have convinced their people that achieving high standards or world class standards is impossible and the people have come to accept it. The people are actually surprised by high standards if they accidentally achieve them. Goussikindey (2006: 11 – 12) puts the point strongly when he observed,

> It is not rare to find out across the continent a road built decades ago without any maintenance. It has to deteriorate entirely before one thinks about replacement. Institutions such as schools, universities, hospitals, are built with money from outside or by an active government but no maintenance will follow. A typical example would be the railway system in most African countries. Very few have been either extended or upgraded since the colonial time when they were built.

Under Belgian rule in the 1960s, the Congo, for example had 88,000 miles of usable road; by 1985 this was doen to 12,000 miles, only 1,400 of them paved (Landes, 2001: 505).

Ten years into the twenty first century, Africa is still 'the dark continent'. The *Economist* edition of 16th August 2007 had this to say about African leadership and electrification of the continent:

Seen from space, Africa at night is unlit – as dark all – but empty Siberia. With nearly 1 billion people, Africa accounts for over a sixth of the world population, but generates only 4 percent of global electricity. Three quarters of that electricity is used by South Africa, Egypt and other countries along the North African littoral.

The need for more power stations in the rest of the continent has been recognized, but most attempts at electrification in the 1970s and 1980s failed. In some countries, dictators pillaged power stations for parts and fuel. In others, power stations were built but not maintained. Turbines were run at full capacity until they broke, then they were abandoned. By some counts, only 17 of Nigeria's 79 power stations, many dating from this period, are still working. The country's demand for power is estimated at 7,600 megawatts against an actual operating capacity of 3, 500 megawatts. The World Bank reckons that 500 million sub-Saharan Africans are without what it calls 'modern energy.

I remember visiting Ghana in 2007. That time in the capital, Accra there were blackouts for twelve hours every day. That situation is not different in many African countries.

Justifying mediocrity is a major disease in Africa. Mediocrity is related to a general lack of ambition to be the best in one's field of endeavor. We are living in a highly competitive world where we are competing not only locally, regionally or continentally, but with the best in the world. We cannot justify our mediocrity by saying it is because we are from Africa – a poor continent. In a globalized world nobody understands that language any more. Individuals have to strive to be best in their fields of endeavor. Nations have to carve out niches and strive to be the best in those areas. When one truly strives to be the best in their field of endeavor success is almost inevitable. By stretching oneself to be the best, one automatically creates the rewards one needs. Opportunities abound for all those who dare stand out of the pack – whether this is for individuals or nations.

Chinua Achebe (1983: 19) summarizes the issue well when he said,

We have displayed a consistent inclination since we assumed management of our own affairs to opt for mediocrity and compromise, to pick a third and fourth eleven to play for us. And as a result: we have always failed and will always fail to make it to the world league. Until, that is, we put merit back on the national agenda.

Short term thinking and immediate gratification

Lack of long term thinking is another shadow Africans have to confront. Many Africans, even professionals do not believe in insurance. It is insurance that other groups have used to create a stronger financial foundation for their future generations. Napoleon Hill once said a man's love for his family can be pretty accurately measured by the amount of life insurance he carries for their protection. By this test many African parents are failures. Most of us in Africa have no financial foundation. Our parents did not leave anything for us and we start life from a scratch and yet we have not yet learnt the lesson because we are repeating the same mistake and our children will not have any foundation.

One would be surprised at the number of people who do not have any wills. When they die they leave pandemonium behind and their property instead of acting as a foundation for the future generations is squandered by opportunists. It is rumored that Mobutu Sese Seko left $ 6 billion in Swiss banks. Because of lack of proper backing documents and a clear will, the Swiss banks now tell us he left only $ 6 million. This mistake is being repeated every day in Africa. Somehow we tend to think we are immortal and that death happens to others but cannot happen to us and therefore we do not need to worry about issues of insurance or wills.

A savings culture is not a value to many Africans. As one Indian put it,

> When I moved to Nairobi from Mombasa eight years ago, I came with nothing. Absolutely nothing. I lived on bananas and a pint of milk a day for two years, putting every shilling into my business. An African would not do that. But I was not afraid to work and I wanted to make money for my children. I will admit the Asians collect money almost as a hobby. We are the Jews of Africa and that's why the Africans resent us (Lamb, 1987: 57).

Building or buying a house and putting one's children through college are two key responsibilities for every parent. These are long term decisions. Many African parents do not make these decisions at all and if they do, it is usually too late. There is a general improvement in buying and building houses though many people still believe that they will build or buy their houses from their pension money. Many parents are still sending their children to very expensive kindergarten schools and buying them designer clothes and toys without having a dime in the bank for their college education. World wide the two critical areas that have continually been increasing in costs are education and health (Drucker, 2002). I remember the time we went to college. That time university education was almost free. We used to pay no fees but a contribution and then the university gave allowances for stationery that equaled our contribution. In addition government gave us travel warrants to travel for free on public transport to and from college. Those days are like a fairy tale from another era now. Parents have to meet all the costs for their children's education. Making early preparations for meeting such costs is a true mark of long term thinking on behalf of the parents. Making such preparations will reduce pressure on the parents when the children reach the college-going ages.

It is also surprising to see people, especially those who are self employed having no any medical schemes. The fact that I have not fallen sick in the 3 past years should not mean I will always be healthy. The probability of needing medical attention increases substantially once one gets married and begins to have children and with one's increasing age (Tofler, 1970). Some people think a medical scheme is a waste of money as they make their monthly contribution when they may not get sick at all. They think a medical scheme may erode their profits but in reality lack of a medical scheme may actually wipe out their entire businesses and in fact their life. Some people have worked so hard to build empires only to discover that those empires were built in the air as there was no foundation of a medical scheme. They ended up paying too dearly and killed their businesses in the process as they had to pay in cash rather than a medical scheme. Some people have actually died unnecessary death because they could not afford the full bills in time of crisis which could be comfortably handled by a medical scheme.

On the other hand, profitability of financial investments is a real challenge in much of Africa. A lot of people who invested money in financial institutions through savings, insurance, treasury bills and bonds in the 1980s which are supposed to have matured by now have nothing to show for it but disappointment. While people are encouraged to shift attitudes towards a more savings culture, the financial institutions also have a challenge to ensure meaningful profitability of people's investments.

It is amazing that up to now we still have leaders on the continent who think they are immortal. They do not see their countries or the continent at a time in the future without them. They believe they will rule forever. These leaders never seem to appreciate the wisdom that *when a reed dries up another one grows in its place.* They are therefore in no urgent mood to create a good legacy for themselves and to create a foundation upon which the next leaders can build. We still have presidents who have ruled for more than three decades and they still want to continue ruling. These individuals are a typical example of the proverb, *the higher the monkey climbs the tree the more its 'ugly parts' become visible.* Leadership is the ability to see into the future long before others see and then to mobilize oneself and people to prepare for and create the desired future. The belief that one is irreplaceable is a key indicator of lack of leadership. Leaders like Julius Nyerere and Nelson Mandela and recently Joachim Chisanu are a still a rare breed on the continent. Leaders like Yoweri Museveni, Robert Mugabe, Abdoulaye Wade and Bakili Muluzi are legion.

Lack of economic patriotism

The other demon to confront is one of lack of economic patriotism. Most Africans tend to love other people more than their own. They would rather patronize other people's businesses rather than the businesses of their own people. They complain that other people have better shops and businesses than they have yet it is they themselves who are making those people have better shops and businesses by patronizing them and not their own people. This is a major hindrance to economic development on the continent and a major explanation why Africans do not own any significant businesses. In any country you go to in Africa, businesses and wealth creating assets are owned by other people and not owners of the land. They are owned by Europeans, Americans, Indians, Japanese and the Chinese. These businesses thrive because of the African's patronage. Africans invest their money into these people's communities and they hardly invest any money into the Africans communities in return. As Chika Onyeani says in his now popular book, *The Capitalist Nigger*, when you invest a dollar into a community, it immediately becomes 8 dollars and within a short time through the multiplier effect it becomes 164 dollars. The way to liberate Africa economically is through what he calls the spider web economic doctrine that is to buy African. By buying African the Africans will be investing their money in their own people on their own continent. This will build economic momentum that will eventually lift the continent up. It makes sense to buy from the others only what our own people cannot supply. This is how Indians in diaspora have managed to make themselves an economic force to reckon with.

On the other hand those African brothers and sisters owning shops and businesses should make sure that they are easy to do business with. Many times the other groups will provide their goods and services at cheaper prices and yet one has to buy the same product from an African's shop at twice the price. Why does one have to feel they are sacrificing when buying from a fellow African? The other groups may use the advantage of larger pools of capital and economies of scale to make their products cheaper but that is where Africans also need to learn the value of cooperative effort and pooling capital together so that they too can provide their services and products at competitive prices. Failure to work together for a bigger good is a colonial hangover that must be overcome. In Africa both the formal and informal value system of colonialism destroyed social solidarity and promoted alienated individualism without social responsibility (Rodney, 1972: 255). This is an explanation why African joint ventures rarely work and why any meaningful wealth creating assets on the continent are owned by foreigners. Rodney (1972: 23) admonishes that so long as foreigners own land, mines, factories, banks, insurance companies, means of transportation, newspapers, power stations, then for so long will the wealth of Africa flow outwards to the hands of those elements. In other words the natural resources and the labor of Africa will continue to produce economic value which is lost to the continent.

Lack of patriotism is also observed in belief and overdependence on expatriates who are often employed to do jobs that locals can ably do. This is one explanation and justification for migration by many young people. They cannot be trusted with meaningful responsibility in their own countries. They therefore leave for the countries that would offer them these opportunities. Paradoxically, they go to fill the jobs left by the expatriates who come to do the work they cannot be entrusted with back in their homes. The mistrust of African leaders of their own local expertise only serves foreign donors well who follow their example mostly with the aim of safeguarding their own interests like creating jobs for their experts and consultants which usually undermines local capacity building efforts. Trust in local expertise and those local experts rising up to the challenge are key elements in locally driven sustainable economic development.

African business owners must avoid greed and opportunistic tendencies of charging unjustifiable prices with the aim of maximizing profit. This is a typical example of short term thinking in business. There are therefore responsibilities on both sides. Africans need to patronize African businesses. We need to buy from others only what our own people cannot supply. Business owners have the responsibility to be easy to do business with. They need to be competitive and they should not think that fellow African's will patronize them even if they are charging exorbitant prices. Many African businesses still have to learn that the customer is king.

Unnecessary dependence, wasteful practices and the culture of not paying back money and things borrowed from friends

Sponging is another challenge constraining economic development on the continent. When one member of a family is trying and is economically better off the whole clan wants to benefit. The person is put under obligation to take care of the whole clan. At the end of the month the whole clan comes with all sorts of bills to the individual. By spreading himself or herself too thinly the person cannot make any significant personal progress. He or she is held back. If one refuses to help, they are branded selfish and unpatriotic. Helping has its place but it should not be at the expense of sustainable personal progress. One must take care of oneself before they can take care of others. Forgetting this makes all help non-developmental. There is such a thing as personal responsibility where every person must take care of themselves and not depend on others.

It is important to always follow ones own agenda even if one may be branded ruthless or inhuman. It is important to strike a balance and as much as possible avoid being sidetracked by others' demands. Personal effort and achievement must be rewarded and it is wrong to think that because we are related those who worked hard to achieve and those who did not must have the same economic status. It is personal and collective effort and achievement that has driven economic development all over the world. But personal effort and achievement cannot be substituted.

One serious demon constraining economic progress among Africans is the culture of not paying back money and other things borrowed from friends. We are very kind and we want to help each other. Sometimes people even use their capital to lend to friends in need but often once they borrow the money it will not be returned. There is this feeling that if he could lend me this money then he must have more. This thinking and practice has led to the demise of many promising businesses. Books, tapes, CDs, DVDs once borrowed usually do not come back. Personally, after many disappointments I have come up with a personal policy that I will not lend anyone any money except to two friends who have never disappointed me and I will follow this policy very religiously. The fastest way to kill businesses and relationships is through borrowing and lending without paying back.

One of the causes of poverty in Africa is diversion of family funds by men to girlfriends and extra marital affairs, a very common practice that is culturally but silently permitted in many African communities.

Weddings and funerals are big economic burdens in Africa. Weddings for common people in Africa are those reserved for princes and princesses in Europe and America. The same is true for funerals. The difference is that the princes and princesses in Europe and America can afford those weddings and funerals while in Africa we can hardly afford without stretching ourselves unnecessarily. The poorest people conduct the most expensive weddings and funerals. Young people are forced to start their married life in deep debt and it will take a long time for them to square the bills incurred for the wedding costs. After losing a member, sometimes a bread winner, families are left much poorer because of costs incurred for funeral costs. In addition to medical costs during the illness, family members will spend money feeding people who come to attend the funeral often for several days. In Africa funerals are not private affairs. The whole community participates. In fact in rural areas and even in many urban areas the economic life of the community comes to a stand still until the funeral is over. And that is not all. Some time after the funeral, there will be a memorial ceremony that will be just as expensive and what with the building of expensive tombstones.

It is important to show respect to the dead but it does not need to be at the expense of the economic well being of the living because after all, the world is for the living! With the AIDS pandemic this is a serious issue as the frequency of deaths is much higher. Modest weddings and funerals would make more economic sense for most people on the continent. In the spirit of ubuntu, weddings and funerals would make economic sense if they were used as opportunities for the young people getting married and bereaved families to use these as 'economic kick starts' with the support from the community rather than burdens that often leave the newly weds and the bereaved poorer.

In the final analysis economic development is about choices and decisions. Africans will have to decide to consciously acknowledge that the continent as a whole is not economically independent and then decide to take corrective action which includes taking responsibility to bring about the needed economic independence (rather than hoping that salvation will come from outside the continent), access or create own wealth creating knowledge and opportunities, begin to own wealth creating assets or businesses rather than leaving these entirely in the hands of foreigners and lastly patronize each others' businesses so that the money they earn and spend can create value on the continent. These are difficult choices and decisions to make but the most difficult of the choices and decisions has to be made at the level of culture and values. Underdevelopment is not a divine order. It is mostly man-made and there is no lack of knowledge as how to eliminate it. The real challenge is cultural and values inertia. As already stated some have gone as far as claiming that underdevelopment is not primarily an economic issue but a cultural one (Rahnema and Bawtree, 1997: 30).

The choice is which values to maintain or adopt because they will help us achieve our goal of economic development and which ones to jettison because though they may have been helpful in the past, they may be standing in the way of our goal of economic development. Giving up long held and cherished cultural values is a key part in the process of economic development. Diamond (2005: 433 – 434) observed that in the last sixty years the world's most powerful countries have given up long held cherished values previously central to their national image while holding to other values. Britain and France abandoned their centuries old role as independently acting world powers; Japan abandoned its military tradition and armed forces; Russia abandoned its long experience with Communism. The United States has retracted substantially though not completely from its former values of racial discrimination, legalized homophobia, a subordinate role of women and sexual repression. Australia is re-evaluating its status as a rural farming society with British identity.

Individually and collectively Africans will need to have the courage to take the decisions to jettison the above discussed negative values and practices and replace them with the positive elements of ubuntu and other cultures that are more supportive to the goal of economic development. The above suggested choices may well be the choice between utopia and oblivion for Africa.

The 'third parent'

Buckminister Fuller (1969) coined the term 'the third parent' to describe the influence of TV in shaping children's values in families. TV and now the Internet are more effective and efficient than most parents in shaping children's values today. Those people who control the media also promote their values. The media today defines what success is. It defines what failure is. The media influences people's aspirations. The media define or suggest morality and ethics. Now through Hollywood there is globalization of values and culture. But the question is what values does Hollywood promote and how congruent are these to our ubuntu culture and values? Does Hollywood promote values such as solidarity, brotherhood, justice and fairness? What values do Hollywood celebrities manifest? What is the influence of those values in shaping human character as understood in Africa?

Through heavy advertising campaigns, people are conditioned to buy what they are told and enticed to buy and not necessarily what they need. Advertising tells people what a good brand is and what a status brand is. TV and now the Internet, being the third parent, influence children who are growing up, absorbing the values coming through what they watch on TV and read on the Internet without questioning. Since the media portrays the West as being more successful, children grow up aspiring to become what they see on the TV and the celebrities they see on the TV. They look down on their parents and elders as being inferior. They look down on them because they do not measure up to the level of material success of their heroes on TV. In this way the foreign media is consciously or unconsciously a tool for influence and control of the developing countries. By giving young people aspirations they have no means to achieve, they keep them chasing a carrot at the end of the stick. Those very few and lucky young people who do become successful, find it difficult to be comfortable with their 'cultural selves'. The television tells young people what current fashion is. It teaches 'modern' marriage and family values. In many countries where illiteracy may be as high as 50 percent, TV values are absorbed wholesale as people have no capacity for critique. What is on TV must be right is a common belief among those people. This is not to say 'the third parent is all negative'. Indeed, the third parent has so many positive aspects and the issue is more to do with being a 'wise consumer'.

In Nigeria during the oil boom and through the influence of Western media the staple food changed from *fufu*, made from yam, to bread, made from imported wheat. More than $ 5 million a month was spent to fly meat to Lagos. Nigeria became the world's largest importer of champagne. They were a proof of the proverb *the person who dips his finger in honey does not do it once.* Ken Saro Wiwa commented,

> Of all the countries who had black gold, Nigeria was the only one that succeeded in doing absolutely nothing with it. The Arabs used their oil very well indeed, not only had they given their people education and a lot else that conduced to good living; they also invested their money in Europe and America. But the Nigerians had invested nothing. Absolutely nothing. They had spent all their money buying foreign food which they consumed or even threw away; in paying for ships waiting on the high seas to deliver food. Somewhere, they just paid out hundreds of millions of dollars for goods or services not delivered (Harden, 1993: 290).

Another example of wholesale copying from Western TV and Internet plus their celebrities is evident in a pop idols program across Africa, one that aims at identifying musical talent on the continent. The contestants are required to compete by singing songs done by pop stars in the West. And these are young people and English is not their first language. There is no lack of musical talent on the continent on which the competition can be based. Very successful musicians have made it using their local languages.

The sad point is that most local media instead of challenging and offering alternative and appropriate values, in trying to catch up with the West, imitate the West and promote the same values. Initiatives like Nollywood in Nigeria have a big and very strategic challenge to make sure they are helping to define and promote what appropriate and development values for the continent should be. It will be very sad if such initiatives also get caught up in trying to be like the Western media and become part of the problem rather than solution to the current values crisis. Sadly today Nollywood glorifies Western values by portraying that everything Western is better than anything local. This is mostly evident in their films portraying urban Nigerian life. Initiatives like Nollywood have great potential to become a more relevant third parent. Such initiatives need to promote a local agenda – that of national and continental economic independence. This notion needs to be entrenched to such an extent that it becomes the natural DNA of every child and individual on the continent. The pervasive power of the media can make a great contribution towards this agenda.

Conclusion

Does culture have a causal effect on economic development? Leading authorities suggest it does (Tabellini, 2006). The positive aspects of ubuntu can form a strong foundation for the continent's economic development. The negative aspects are responsible for much of the arrest of economic development on the continent. Ubuntu has not really failed to form a foundation for economic development but rather it has not been given a chance. Investing in building on the positive elements of ubuntu and reversing the negative aspects of ubuntu should form part of the strategy in the economic recovery of the continent. So far the link between culture and economic development has not been fully appreciated. The failure of the mid-sixties and early seventies idea of 'transfer of technology' to Africa as a way to boost its productivity and 'catch up' with industrialization and many other previous efforts failed, among many other reasons, because they failed to take into account the negative cultural practices discussed above (Goussikindy, 2006: 12).

Given the bleak prospects of the continent and the evidence that culture can play a key role in economic development, there is a great need to consciously revolutionalize the culture of the continent so that it becomes more supportive rather than a hindrance to economic development. Economic miracles of success stories like Singapore have been built on an economically empowering culture based on talent, initiative, adventure, endeavor, risk, confidence and rigor; and savings and investment (Yew, 2000: 381). Africa would do well to transform its culture by managing migration and ensuring it is economically beneficial to the continent, the courage to speak out when things go wrong, emphasize quality and high standards, encourage long term thinking, patriotism and eliminating selfish and wasteful practices.

Just as *the owner of the smell does not notice it* we are mostly unconscious of the shadows of our culture and how they are keeping the continent from moving towards economic independence. It is time we became more conscious and confronted these shadows head on.

Once more, this chapter does not claim that ubuntu is the solution to Africa's economic underdevelopment but that its omission in economic development efforts is a major explanation of the failure of those efforts. By putting aside the positive elements of our culture we have disconnected ourselves from who we are because *the river that forgets its source soon dries up.*

CHAPTER 7: WHAT CAN AFRICA LEARN FROM SOUTH KOREA'S ECONOMIC MIRACLE?

Introduction

It is not the intention of this book to go into detailed case studies of how other countries and regions have demonstrated that it is possible to gain economic independence mostly through self-effort. The stories of Malaysia, Singapore, Mauritius and Botswana provide ample evidence and they are well documented elsewhere. This chapter will present one case study of South Korea and then draw lessons that will be compared with general lessons from the aforementioned countries to tease out a general strategy that they followed to gain their economic independence while fully recognizing that generalizations may not be possible. The lessons learnt can provide a general direction that can be followed and indeed be fine-tuned to fit local context if the African countries and the continent as a whole are to gain economic independence. Learning from what has worked elsewhere has the advantage of enabling people to draw lessons from real experience rather than just mere theories. Lee Kuan Yew (2000: 687 – 688) emphasizes the point well when he states:

> If there was one formula for our success, it was that we were constantly studying how to make things work, or how to make them work better. I was never a prisoner of any theory. What guided me was reason and reality. The acid test I applied to every theory or scheme was, would it work? This was the golden thread that ran through my years in office. If it did not work or if the results were poor, I did not waste much time and resources on it. I almost never made the same mistake twice and I tried to learn from the mistakes others had made. I discovered early in office that that there were few problems confronting me in government that other governments had not met and solved. So I made the practice of finding out who else had met the problems we faced, how they had tackled it and how successful had they been…I would send a team of officers to visit and study those countries that had done it well. I preferred to climb on the shoulders of others who had gone before us.
>
> I learned to ignore criticism and advice from experts and quasi-experts, especially academics in the social and political sciences. They have petty theories on how society should develop to approximate their ideal, especially how poverty should be reduced and welfare extended. After everything had been analyzed and argued, I went by my gut instinct of what would work in Singapore

It is important to note however that by suggesting that we can learn from individual countries like South Korea, we should not get under the impression that the forces keeping an entire continent in inertia can be resolved by individual country efforts. Castro (2008: 389) observes,

> People struggle against under development, disease, illiteracy but what we might call the global solution to humanity's problems has not yet been found. Humanity's problems cannot be solved on a basis of individual nations, because today more than ever before, domination is achieved on a global basis .

. . the WTO (World Trade Organization), the World Bank, the International Monetary Fund establish the rules for a situation of *de facto* domination and exploitation which is equal or worse than the most dreadful consequences of colonial slavery.

This is where international civil society, if it is really worthy its salt, needs to spend 90% of its energy and effort. If the aid system is real, correcting the above situation is where they should be investing their energy and attention.

The South Korean economic development miracle

One of the most extra-ordinary economic development stories in recent history is the transformation of South Korea from one of the poorest countries on earth to a modern industrialized economy is less than half a century. South Korea in the 1950s was considered a hopeless development fledgling (Mehrotra and Jolly, 1998: 433). Within a generation, Korea has managed to build from almost nothing world class export industries and the best educated workforce in the developing world. This has enabled South Korea to participate effectively in the globalized world. Korea got a lot of financial aid especially from the United States.

In 1960, South Korea's GDP of $2.3 billion and per capita income of $79 were among the lowest in the world. In 2005, the income of the average South Korean had risen to $16, 800, a thirty-fold increase since 1960 and was rated thirty-sixth in the world. The GDP reached $ 800 billion. This was rated number 10 and represented a fifty fold increase.

In comparison to Africa, an illustration with a country like Ghana, which is considered by many to be a relatively successful African country, will illustrate the point well. In the 1960s Ghana and South Korea had similar per capita incomes but now the average South Korean has 27 times the income of the average Ghanaian. Korea has become the 13th wealthiest nation in the world and Ghana remains among the poorest.

Korea's achievement was mostly home grown. Korea has been termed a 'developmental dictatorship' and the leaders decreed most of the terms of economic development like orders of a military campaign. All leaders and governments from 1953 were consistently committed to economic changes that improved the lives of most Koreans. This was despite differences in their ideologies or policies. In the 1970s the President re-issued the book *The Art of War* in a different version that depicted economic competition as a war won by achieving a dominant market share. The government established large companies that were seen as artillery for the economic war. The leaders instituted universal primary and secondary education and invested heavily in the country's basic infrastructure. The leaders arrested hundreds of business leaders for corruption, imposed huge fines. One President, Park Chung Lee told the arrested business people that they would pay their fines by investing their assets in a number of labor intensive light industries. To effect this he created a system of loans, tax breaks, and bureaucratic favors for businesses. This propelled the country's industrialization.

Some extreme leaders like General Chun Doo Hwan and Roh Tae Woo declared martial law, and declared the arrests and executions of thousands of political activists, banned political activity and actually closed universities and they turned to economic reforms that strengthened the industrialization drive and expanded domestic businesses for Korea's emerging new consumer class.

The basic strategy that Korea used: jump starting some selected industries by giving them a more favorable environment like tax breaks, huge loans and government contracts or favors was copied from Japan. But in contrast to Japan, South Korea invested more in developing local businesses. The local companies manufactured for export. Government made it illegal for Koreans to purchase many of the products intended for export including radios, TV and telephones. Imports were equally regulated. Korea in contrast to India and China did not import a modern industrial base by inviting foreign companies from developed countries. Singapore developed its own base.

Since the 1970s, South Korea has devoted most of its GDP to business investments. So when world events created opportunities Korean companies have always been ready to seize the moment. Today fourteen of the world's five hundred largest companies in the world are South Korean beating Spain, Sweden, Italy, India; and Singapore, Thailand and Taiwan combined.

Secondly, Since the 1960s South Korea devoted its GDP to education at an average of 10% per year. This is much higher than any other developing country and even most of the developed countries. Today 40% of the country's high school students and 80% of its college students attend private schools, the highest percentage in the world. Creating one of the world's most highly educated workforces. This has enabled Korea to competitively participate in the globalized world. The high education levels has made Korea one of the most equal developing society. Today Korea is ranked the eleventh most equal society in the world beating France, Italy, Great Britain and the United States.

The crisis of 1980: world wide oil shock, the worst harvest in a generation, mass unrest following the assassination of President Park and the re-establishment of military rule brought the country's economy to a complete halt. This led to a series of new reforms: breaking some of the huge companies into smaller units and phasing out unprofitable subsidiaries, cutting export subsidies so the businesses would focus more on the domestic market. In addition Korean companies were encouraged to develop their own advanced technologies and innovations. By 2000 Korea was investing more of its GDP in Research and Development – 2.4% than all but eight countries. More significantly government decreed an increase (35%) in allocation of bank loans to local businesses. With these changes, within a decade smaller enterprises accounted for nearly half of all Korean manufacturing.

The 1997 – 1998 crisis was the next to hit Korea. In one year the country's GDP shrank by nearly 7% with the currency losing half its value, unemployment tripling from 3% to 9%. It took a $57billion bailout from the IMF to stabilize the currency and the financial system. The conditions for the bail out were to open up competition to western companies and breaking up further the large conglomerates in South Korea. Half of the major conglomerates disappeared within two years and the Korean economy rebounded with a 9.5 percent growth in 1999 and 8.5% percent in 2000. Foreign investors came in large numbers to buy local businesses leading to foreign companies owning more than 40% of the companies listed on the Seoul Stock Exchange.

Growth since 2000 has averaged more than 4.5 percent per year with productivity rising at 4.3 percent a year. Unemployment has remained less than 4%. In 2005, 80% of households had access to home computers beating the United States, Britain, France, or Germany. In the same year two thirds of South Koreans used the Internet. Western companies prefer investing in South Korea because it provides a workforce and customer base that is already computer and Internet literate plus the infrastructure to plug in their global networks. Korea's success can and should become a model for African countries who are mostly at the same stage Korea was in the 1960s.

Finally, Korea's success was based on massive public and private investments in education and health care, large initial subsidies for core industries accompanied by low barriers to imports and foreign competition, substantial social protections which, like the industrial subsidies, phase down, and support for entrepreneurship. It relied on authoritarian politics with prospects of a transition to a democracy (Mehrotra and Jolly, 1998: 265).

The *Art of War* emphasizes the importance of attacking and defeating the enemy by strategy. It states that, "the skillful leader subdues the enemy's troops without any fighting; he captures their cities without laying siege on them; he overthrows their kingdom without lengthy operations in the field. With his forces intact he will dispute the mastery of the empire without losing a man, his triumph will be complete" (Clavell, 19981:19). Using this principle in economic terms South Korea and the other Asian Tigers have conquered a world order that had destined them to become poor third world countries and carve an economic niche for themselves where they can exercise power.

According to Chika Onyeani (2000: 31), using the concept of spider web doctrine, East Indians in America have managed to take over the newsstand business in New York and other large cities in America, the taxi business, travel agencies; the motel and hotel businesses not forgetting the gas stations. In their assault on corporate America, they did not have to fight using physical weapons. They did not worry about an unfair world order. They did not complain. They did not do demonstrations. They just went to work. They devised a powerful strategy and began to implement it for real, one step at a time. They did not wait for aid. Their strategy is built on cooperation and living arrangements as a people. They eat only their food, they do not buy from outsiders. They spend all the money they make within their communities. Whatever money they make circulates within their community. They do not live beyond their means. They can have up to 20 people living in one house with the aim of using the money saved from rentals as start up capital for the next person until each one of them has a business of their own. As ardent believers in life insurance, they use the money accruing after parents' death to reinvest in their family businesses for more capital and jobs for their people. This is why the majority of them work for themselves or other East Indian companies. In short, within three decades the

East Indians waged war on corporate America and carved a niche for themselves where they now exercise power. They implemented their strategy silently, no one noticed what was happening until their victory was complete.

What Africa can learn from South Korea

Recognition that development is always self-development
Despite getting massive aid from the United States, the leaders in South Korea knew that real development comes from own wealth creation. They knew that development is always self development. This is why the government established its own companies and has consistently devoted most of its GDP to business investments.

Visions of aspiration
South Korea was fortunate to have visionary leaders despite their dictatorial tendencies. Taking a war model to business, they were able to launch an attack on the corporate world with the aim of establishing their space in their world. It is also important to note that each succeeding leader built on the efforts of the previous leader. This is often not the case in most of Africa. Often the new leader will spend much of their time destroying what his or her predecessor built and very little time in building their own that the next leader will also destroy. The leaders were courageous in dealing with corruption which is usually not the case in Africa. Much of the anti-corruption drive on the continent is mere lip service. Economic development takes time. It requires vision, leadership, consistency and courage to confront obstacles like corruption.

Investment in wealth creating knowledge
Wealth is natural resources compounded by intellect's know how. South Korea was not as blessed as Africa with natural resources but this did not deter the country from developing. Relying heavily on 'intellect's know how' South Korea maximized the transformation of the little resources they had in the country and imported what they did not have. This was made possible by the governments decision to invest heavily in education, especially higher education and technical know how. It was also made possible by the decision to make available to as many people as possible computers and the internet.

Owning businesses
A strong point in South Korea's strategy was in promoting own local businesses through tax breaks, soft loans and giving them government contracts. This was key to South Korea's success because local businesses invest and use their profits in the country where as foreign companies send their profits to the countries they come from. When South Korea opened to foreign companies, these found the local companies already strong enough to compete favorably with them. This is the way South Korea dealt with the complex problem facing local businesses: barriers to entry, lack of finance and leg up competitive

advantage held by foreign countries after keeping the local companies in Africa, for example, out of the game for over 500 years.

In addition, they were visionary enough to focus not only on producing for domestic consumption but also carving a niche in the global market. A key lesson in the words of Handy (2006: 198) is that the South Korean leaders recognized that what they had was a 'flea' economy and that they needed to ride on the back of some elephant. In other words the local economy was too small to create wealth and they rode on the American economy and markets.

Patronizing own businesses

When foreign companies came to Korea they found that loyalty ties between the people and their companies were already established. In much of Africa businesses have been conducted by Indians and other races. When an African sets up a business he or she has an uphill task to break the stereotype that black people are not good business people. This makes it difficult to attract sustainable patronage. Buying from local businesses has the advantage that the money paid to the companies will be used within the same country and therefore improving the country's economy.

The story of South Korea above and the story of Singapore as narrated by Lee Kuan Yew in his book *From Third World to First World: the Story of Singapore* clearly demonstrate the importance of the above lessons in shifting from economic dependence to economic independence. These and other countries that have made the shift have shown the importance of recognizing that political independence is not the same as economic independence, and the need for visions of aspiration, the critical importance of wealth creating knowledge. They have also demonstrated the importance of building and cultivating business power as an engine for economic growth, the ability to attract foreign businesses and more importantly, to develop local parallel businesses alongside the foreign businesses. Related to the foregoing, they have shown the importance of the ability to create services and products that can compete favorably on the global market.

Conclusion

Japan gave up the war of weaponry and engaged in the war for economic independence and supremacy. South Korean leaders used the book *The Art of War* to craft their financial independence strategies. Singapore knew it was surrounded by hostile enemies intent to see them fall which they used as motivation to build economic power as a geopolitical strategy. This is what these countries did to gain their economic independence. This is also what Africa must do.

In colonial times the enemy was the colonialists, in the fight for multiparty democracy the enemy was our own dictators. In the war for economic independence the enemy is much more formidable for he or she is us. We see at the same time when we look in the mirror our best ally and our worst enemy. The war for economic independence is so formidable because it requires conquering the individual and collective self. It is very easy to point fingers of blame at outside factors and how other people are keeping us where we are. It takes real maturity to be men and women enough to acknowledge that we are actually the problem and also the solution and that we can only be our own liberators like the people of South Korea, Singapore, Japan and other countries have managed to demonstrate. Like in China they have extension workers who are called 'poverty fighting officers', I think every African ought to become a 'poverty fighting officer'.

It is important to see what others have achieved to have a sense of what is possible because *to one who has never traveled a small garden is a forest* and *the eyes that have seen an ocean cannot be satisfied with a mere lagoon.* Many African leaders have managed to convince their people that economic independence is impossible. But countries like South Korea, Singapore, Mauritius and Botswana have proved that those leaders are wrong and if many people are made to see the possibilities these countries have achieved, they will not be satisfied to continue being where they are today. One of the biggest hindrances to development in Africa is lack of role models that can help raise the bar of people's expectations. These countries are the 'oceans' and 'forests' that can raise the people's bar.

CHAPTER 8: POSITIONING AFRICA IN THE WORLD

Introduction

The world is going through a transition. It is shifting from being primarily a uni-polar to a multi-polar world. The Rise of Asia, especially China and India, is shifting power from being purely concentrated in one super power to being shared with the emerging powers as well. From a developmental point of view all social systems grow and develop through three distinct stages or phases. These are the dependent, independent and inter-dependent phases. The world is shifting from an independent to an inter-dependent stage of development (Livegoed, 1969; 1973 and Kaplan, 1996: 15). A shift from one stage of development to the other is often characterized by a major crisis or crises.

Africa is generally struggling with the crisis of shifting from the dependent stage to the independent stage as it is clear the continent is not yet truly economically, politically, culturally and technologically independent. The developed world, with the rise of Asia is under a crisis to shift from the independent to the inter-dependent stage. The Western countries are relatively economically, politically, culturally and technologically independent. This has managed to propel their economic growth to unprecedented levels. But unsustainable growth cannot go on forever. The 'credit crunch' is a clear proof for this. This is why a purely economic approach – bailing out failed companies- will not work. The most important thing is to realize that the financial crisis and other crises like environmental degradation, climate change, rising food prices and increasing fear and anxiety among people are just symptoms of the need of an end of an era and the beginning of a transition to a new beginning in the era of true inter-dependence.

Strategically, there is a real danger to focus on solving the current symptoms and lose strategic sight in the need to facilitate the emergence of the new era – the age of true interdependence. It is interesting to note that the call for this shift is happening a decade into the new century because it is believed that every 100 years a significant shift happens in the world. Western countries have lived in the age of mass intelligence signaled by the shift to the industrial era about a 100 years ago and entrenched by the information technology era. Now there is a call to more beyond mere intelligence to wisdom or to move from the age of knowledge to the age of wisdom. The question is – do we have the leadership that is visionary, capable and humble enough to lead the way? And where will that leadership come from?

Implications for Africa

Three possible scenarios present themselves for Africa. Being donor-dependent, Africa may brace for tougher times because the donor countries may want to concentrate on solving their domestic problems first. Like one preacher told me the other day, the scripture, Love your neighbor as you love yourself, may mean that you must love yourself first before you can understand how to love your neighbor. This is an expected route that Western countries may take and it is completely understandable.

Another likely route, though not very likely, is that in their strategies to resolve the current crisis Western countries will be wise enough to realize that the 'African problem' is part and parcel of the current global crisis and that excluding it from the proposed solutions will only undermine those efforts eventually. This may offer an opportunity to rethink why after 50 years the aid system has failed to lift Africa out of poverty and economic dependence and what more effective forms of help should look like.

The last route and I would say the most developmental one for Africa is to be proactive – not to sit down and watch how Western countries will resolve 'their' crises. It is our crisis as well since we all inhabit the same global village. Being proactive means being able to tell the world that Africa can and should make a contribution towards resolving the crises. And that contribution can be our ubuntu culture. I was very encouraged when I was invited to the Desmond Tutu Foundation in London. They are planning to work with the youths in the UK on leadership and community development using the principles of ubuntu. This is the first initiative that has taken an African concept to use in Western societies. I am sure this initiative will draw a lot of attention and its success would signal significant shift towards interdependence.

Globalization and the rise of China

Two major forces are combining today to shape the immediate and long term future of the world. These are globalization and the rise of China and India as major geopolitical forces. Globalization refers to the integrative ever increasing speed of doing business among the nations and regions of the world. It simply means each individual, business or country are not in competition only locally any more but with the rest and the best in the world. In a globalized world competition can come from anywhere on earth any time. The challenge in a globalized world is to strive to be the best and to position oneself globally. Globalization implies the removal of national and regional boundaries and the creation of a borderless economy where the rule is survival of the fittest. The internet is playing a key role in driving globalization.

Globalization simply means a product will arrive on your doorstep from another country or region cheaper than it takes to produce it in your own country. The challenge of globalization is therefore twofold: Can you produce the same product or even a better one and sell it cheaper than the one from the other country? The second challenge is, if you do not have the comparative advantage to produce it cheaper, what product can you produce using your comparative advantage that you can export and will arrive in another country cheaper than they can produce it there or cheaper than any similar product from any other country? Both these challenges require knowledge and brain power. This is where China becomes a formidable force because they have unmatched capacity for mass production of cheap commodities. Globalization is reorganizing the world. Those people, countries and continents that have something of value to offer at a better price and quality than the others will rise while those that do not will sink like a stone. In the globalized world and the world of the internet, national boundaries do not matter anymore.

China has a population of a billion plus people. The population of China is bigger than the population of the entire continent of Africa! Within its boundaries China does not produce all the resources it needs. As a steadily prospering economy China will need to import petroleum, food and other basic needs to satisfy its one billion people. The rise in imports in China has created shortage of the same commodities on the world market leading to sharp rises in food prices and petroleum, for example. As China and India continue to gain momentum these trends are likely to be with us for the foreseeable future. In fact, we can rightly say even if there will be some interventions to correct the situation, the era of cheap food is gone. We are in another era now.

Both globalization and the rise of China are major forces that are shaping the future of the world in general and that of Africa in particular. These forces offer both actual and potential opportunities and threats to the continent. How they will shape the future of the continent depends to a large extent on how Africa deals with its current economical, technological, political and cultural challenges discussed in the previous chapters. Strategically positioning Africa in the increasingly globalized world with increasing costs of commodities will require a strategy based on striking a balance on the continent's doing, relating and being.

Globalization is here to stay. The increasing influence of the digital age is evidence enough that globalization is here to stay. According to Govindarajan and Gupta (2001: 15), the digital age refers to the following trends: convergence between computing and communications technologies and the spread of the internet, on going increase in the power of the computing and communications technologies coupled with an on-going decline in the cost of these technologies, emergence of point and click interfaces that are based on open standards, are cheap to set up and run and are global; the roll out of broad band communications technologies; and the on-going explosive growth in mobile communications in developed as well as developing regions of the world. Globalization is here to stay and the only wise response is not to wish it away but to rise up to the challenge and create one's opportunities by identifying one's uniqueness and cultivating a niche around it on which to exercise power and influence.

What should Africa do?

Globalization assumes a level playing ground especially in infrastructure and telecommunications. On an average, currency to the level of 2 trillion dollars exchanges hands daily in the world (Schwab, 2001: 131). But very few of those dollars pass through or land in Africa, the main reason being lack of infrastructure and efficient telecommunications.

As already stated, all natural systems go through three stages of development. These are the dependent, independent and inter-dependent stages. Being natural systems, the same is true for societies. Dependent societies are characterized by insufficient and inefficient economic, political, technological and cultural systems and infrastructure. They are also characterized by higher dependence on individual leaders or failure to remove from power leaders they are not happy with. Dependent systems cannot sustain themselves. They have to depend on others for their continued survival. In a more blunt expression, they are at the mercy of other societies for their continued survival.

Just as there is nothing wrong in being a child, there is nothing wrong in being in a dependent stage. The problem comes when one is a child for too long – when one has growth and development impediments. The problem comes when one is still a child when they are supposed to be a grown up. Africa is a case in point. We have been a child for too long and there is a lot of catching up that we have to do. Globalization signifies that we are now living in an inter-dependent era where value comes from synergy created by independent entities. Synergy means each party is contributing something that the other party needs. Globalization is a game of adults playing an adult-to-adult game and not adult-to-children games. Africa today is out of place because it is not contributing anything to the game, at least not in significant enough levels to result in her own continental economic shift. Of all the brands on the world market, African brands can be counted on the fingers of one hand and even much less. Fifty years after independence this is a pathetic situation indeed.

The most urgent need in Africa now is to invest in infrastructure and systems that can support economic, political, technological and cultural development. These are the levers for playing in a globalized world. Without good roads, electricity, efficient telecommunications, improved health and education facilities it is impossible to be an effective player in the globalized world. Globalization depends on speed and efficiency. Much of Africa is still too slow and inefficient to play in the globalized world. If one goes to the bank or public hospital they take up to the whole day to be served if you will be served at all. If you go to immigration and road traffic offices, you will need weeks to be served. You are lucky to have electricity for the whole day and you are fortunate if water will be running. Speed and efficiency can be gained by investing in the above areas. How much of the aid today is directed at making significant improvements in the above areas to an extent that will enable Africa to be a competent player in the globalized world? Phone connections between neighboring countries are still connected through countries in Europe. You have to pay the moon and the earth to make phone calls to Europe or America from Africa.

There is need to invest in wealth creating knowledge management at individual, organizational, national and continental levels. Much of the curricula on the continent need to be revisited. Much of what is learnt in schools is still aimed at creating the 'employee mind' and not 'the problem solver or entrepreneur mind' who can, by solving the above problems, generate wealth for the continent. Evidence to this is that up to now there is no African billionaire (I mean black African) while paradoxically African professionals are among the most highly qualified in the world.

There is need for more individuals to get interested and involved in politics and not leaving the arena of politics to the politicians alone. The practice of politics has become more of a curse than a blessing in most parts of Africa. People are enduring their political leaders as a heavy burden. Their death (which is their only hoped for exit strategy) is often a great relief to the people. Poor politics create poor economics. Investment in political development and consciousness is therefore supposed to be a major priority in Africa today.

Just like I have written chapters on Africa's economy, politics and culture, I planned to write a chapter on Africa's technology. I was surprised to find out that I had nothing to write on Africa's technology because Africa does not produce anything as far as technology is concerned.

It is through technology that resources are turned into wealth but Africa today is a consumer of technology and not a producer. Technology is the major force driving the globalization agenda. It is very surprising how an entire continent can allow itself to be a consumer and not a producer and yet have some of the most qualified engineers in the world! Where are the engineers and what are are they doing? How can we still hope for the future of the continent in a globalized world driven by technology when we have no technological contribution at all? If there is an area that needs serious soul searching today, it is technology. We still import tooth picks, pins, threads, just imagine. As long as we are totally dependent technologically we should forget about the future. Governments have a big challenge to create enabling environments for our engineers to use their brains to create technologies that this continent needs and that the continent can export to other continents.

A Roman Catholic archbishop in Mozambique once alleged that he had information that there was a conspiracy by the West to wipe out the black race especially the Africans through biological warfare. President Gadafi of Libya made the same allegation though he said the West would use economic strategies to recolonize Africa. If such allegations were true, how prepared technologically are we as a people to defend ourselves? The answer is obvious and implications are grave.

There is need for a cultural revival in Africa – the pride in being African. At least we have an identifiable culture that we can cultivate back into our society. This is the ubuntu culture and its principles:
- Sharing and collective ownership of opportunities, responsibilities and challenges
- The importance of people and relationships over things
- Participatory decision making and leadership
- Patriotism and loyalty; and
- Reconciliation as a goal of conflict management

A cultural revival of the above principles would form a very strong foundation upon which to build our global position as a people. Ubuntu and its principles need to find a way into the school curricula from as early an age as possible. We need to find ways to integrate these into our institutions and businesses as a basis for competitive edge. In a world where human relationships have been put in the background in favor of profit, the conscious practice of ubuntu would give Africa a very strong competitive edge. It would enable Africa to participate in globalization with a human face which is currently a big challenge.

The Japanese made money selling 'Japanese culture' to the corporate world. The Chinese are making money selling Chinese culture to the corporate world. If we can demonstrate that our culture is an asset and can be used as tool to improve corporate performance we can also sell it to the global corporate world especially to the West where individualism is the norm.

As stated above, I was very much delighted, while on a fellowship in the UK, when I was invited to the Desmond Tutu 'Ubuntu' Foundation offices in London. The organization is implementing leadership development initiatives among the youths in the UK using ubuntu principles as its framework. In my experience, this is a first initiative I have seen that has taken an African concept to apply in a European context.

The financial global crisis of 2008 will require a debate on new values for capitalism and globalization. Africa needs to be proactive in making contribution towards this debate because 'ubuntu' offers a significant contribution towards this debate and towards the creation of a more sustainable and humane world.

In a world of increasing food prices, it is very clear that a niche that Africa can carve for itself is to be the bread basket of the world. As a result of the rising food crisis many countries are already experiencing the reversal of decades of economic progress and 100 million people are being pushed back into absolute poverty (Africa Progress Report, 2008: 4). As Kwame Nkrumah said, the DRC alone, if properly managed can produce enough food for the entire continent and surplus for exporting outside the continent. Proposals have already been made by the United Nations, for example, to invest more in agriculture in Africa as a way of dealing with the global problem of rising food prices. To make sure this helps lift the continent it will require to think in terms of a revolution like the green revolution of Asia. This will involve investments in key inputs such as fertilizer, improved seeds, effective water management, new crop varieties and linking the farmers to markets through investments in roads and other types of infrastructure.

It will also be important to make sure that instead of producing and exporting raw grains, it will be necessary to export finished products. Our agriculturists need to find more appropriate low external input sustainable technologies so that we can minimize the cost of inputs and maximize outputs. If there was ever a time for African agriculturists to show the world the type of stuff they are made of, this is. This is the time for African agriculturists to stand up and be counted. Agriculture today has gained a very strategic position as a lever for economic empowerment. I know of only one nobel prize to Africa on science that was given to Wangaari Mathaai of Kenya. Maybe solving the problem of the rising costs of food could give Africa another opportunity for such a level of recognition. Government could help in creating an enabling environment but this is an arena of entrepreneurs. We need young and ambitious people who can put their brains together, get loans from banks or better still grants from government and go to work.

In addition to creating or carving a niche for Africa this would also create employment for so many people. The Chinese and the Japanese may sell us their gadgets and we will sell them food. This is leveling the playing ground in globalization. This way we will be able to play the adult-to-adult game rather than the current adult-to-child game of aid. Contributing towards the world food shortage could be Africa's greatest opportunity in the globalized world.

How should Africa relate?

I am a very strong believer in the law of invitation. That is to say when you have something of value you will be needed and others will want to associate with you. If you do not, you will be avoided and they will not want to associate with you. A proverb says *failure is an orphan but success has many relatives.* People do not want to associate with someone who has nothing to offer. Africa today is an orphan and a burden and therefore does not have many friends or relatives. In the relationships that Africa is involved she is mostly a beggar. Ensuring effective relationships has first and foremost to do with developing one's value.

President Kwame Nkrumah and Gadafi of Libya fought very hard for the unification of Africa into the United States of Africa. In the words of President Gadafi,"Africa should build one federal government as soon as possible. Africa should have one identity, one nationality, one people, one currency, one army…this will be the birth of the black giant."

This bid has been rejected. From an institutional development point of view this is understandable because interdependence which the United States of Africa would imply is only possible if the constituent entities are independent. The United States of Africa is not possible today because the constituent countries are still at the dependent stage of development. Dependent countries cannot cooperate in an interdependent way. This is why marriage is for adults and not children because first and foremost marriage implies responsibility. We cannot expect children to demonstrate the responsibility required to run successful marriages and families. Similarly we cannot expect dependent countries to demonstrate the responsibility required to run such a strategic entity as the United States of Africa.

A United States of Africa will only be possible when a critical mass of countries on the continent become truly independent. Today no country in Sub-Sahara Africa except may be for South Africa and Botswana can claim to be truly independent. What is worrying is that between Kwame Nkrumah and President Gadafi, there is a period of fifty years and we are still not ready. Shall we get ready at all to make the United States of Africa a reality? The balkanization or division of Africa into the countries that now exist (many of which have no geopolitical significance) was a typical example of the divide and rule principle. Unity through the United States of Africa could be Africa's only hope of meaningfully playing in the globalized world. This will be possible because then the continent can speak with one voice and it will be possible to take more control of its natural resources. What is happening today is if some outsiders come to one country and offer exploitive conditions for business, if that country refuses, they simply go to the next more desperate country and get what they want. The cumulative effect is one of weakening the continent as the proverb says *when locusts fight it is the crow who feasts.* This lack of unity just creates opportunities for others to continue exploiting the continent.

Every African, at whatever stage of development need to be taught and challenged on their responsibility to the development of the continent. When individuals are taking responsibility to the development of their communities, countries and the continent, the continent will rise to a higher level of recognition on the global scene. When each country identifies its comparative advantage or niche, the most important thing will be to increase intra-continental trade. Today intra-continental trade is at the level of only 4% . This takes us back to Chika Onyeani's spider web economic doctrine. The more we invest in others' economies, the more we sponsor their prosperity and decapitalize ourselves. If we can invest more in each other's economy on the continent, we can build our continental wealth and power more.

As we build national niches it will become possible to create viable continental unity and institutions that are endogenously supported and can therefore create a continental voice on the globe. I do not understand how continental institutions that are supposed to represent the African voice can truly speak with an African voice when they are funded by the same people they are supposed to challenge. This is naivety. The greatest task for these institutions is to fight for the control of Africa's resources by Africans and not outsiders and building the capacity of the continent to produce finished products and services that Africa can offer on the world market. Anything apart from this is just skirting around the real issue with the danger of such institutions becoming more of part of the African economic problem than the solution.

What should Africa be?

An entity's doing cannot exceed its being. In fact an entity will use resources allocated to it up to the level of its being or capacity and the rest will be wasted. The aid that comes to Africa is used only up to the level of the countries' and continent's capacity and the rest is wasted. To measure the capacity of the country or the continent one just has to observe where the aid has gone.

The being of an entity mostly has to do with its culture. Can people, especially grown ups be taught new values? I don't know but I know that every person on earth wants a better life for himself or herself first and then their family. In fact progress is the mode of humanity. This is the basis upon which we hope for human progress.

Repositioning Africa will have to do with containing our brain power by reducing brain drain or migration, confronting issues and giving each other constructive negative feedback, raising standards, improving our long term thinking, avoiding jealous and supporting one another.

In an era when knowledge and brain power are the most important resource, brain drain is the greatest assault on the continent. Patriotism is a key need among African professionals. Those Africans who have migrated need to make the economic liberation of the continent their major occupation. Every professional in diaspora need to ask themselves what they are doing to make a contribution towards the economic liberation of the continent.

We need to develop capacity to say no to wrong things especially from our leaders. We need to learn to demand accountability on the decisions and actions of our leaders. We also need to be informed about what is happening in the other parts of the continent and be concerned enough with the issues our brothers and sisters are facing because Africa is one. What happens in one part of the continent affects all of us. Darfur and Zimbabwe, for example, are African and not national issues needing the attention and action of all Africans. If our leaders are silent, we as citizens need to apply pressure on them to take a clear stand in condemning such acts.

In Africa we have normalized wrong things: black outs are wrong, water not coming out of the faucets is wrong, telephones that do not work is wrong, buses and airplanes that do not come or leave on time is wrong, leaders that do not fulfill their promises are wrong and all these must be challenged. I am particularly concerned now that many African countries have had their debts cancelled. This is expected to usher the continent to a new era of economic progress but I am not convinced about the mechanisms put in place in many African countries to monitor if such a shift will indeed take place. Can we begin to show where the money gained through debt relief is going? Africa owed the West 375 billion dollars and we cannot show where the money went. Are we going to show where the debt relief money is going or it will be the same story?

Singapore transformed itself from a typical third world country to a first world country in 25 years by following two key strategies. These were:

- Leap frogging their hostile region and linking up with the developed world (through trade not aid) – America, Europe and Japan – and attract their manufacturers to produce in Singapore and export their products to the developed countries.
- Create a first world class oasis in a third world region. This meant training people and equipping them to provide first world standards of service with the help of schools, trade unions, community centers and social organizations.

Following the two strategies, Singapore has managed to transform itself into a typical first world country and a force to be reckoned with on the global scene. Singapore prepared itself for a globalized world long before globalization became a conscious concept. There is need to improve and invest more in the role of standard setting bodies in Africa. There is need to enlist the support of schools, trade unions and social organizations in cultivating a standards culture on the continent.

In addition to government and the other institutions, a standards culture is mostly a personal responsibility. As individuals we need to raise the bar to enable us to compete with the best in the world in our different fields of endeavor. If we can do it in sports, we can surely do it in other fields of endeavor as well.

As Africans we believe that a person's primary responsibilities are towards his family – children, spouse, parents and siblings. Long term thinking means making arrangements in advance for these people. This includes college education for children, life insurance, writing a will and having a medical scheme. Many times we have upside down priorities. We spend our hard earned money on immediate gratification at the expense of creating a formation for a more comfortable future. We send our children to the most expensive kindergarten schools when we do not have any money in the account for their college education. We buy them designer clothes and toys when no arrangement for their future has been made.

Long term thinking implies acceptance of our mortality and dispensability as facts and therefore the need to build capacity of those who will inevitably take over from us. For argument's sake, take two shops for example – one belonging to an African and the other belonging to an Indian. If both the Indian and African die, most likely the Indian's shop will go on and may be even stronger than when the owner was alive. The African's shop will most likely follow the owner. The reason is the Indian taught his children how to run the shop from as an early age as possible because he knew one day he would die but his family would still need the shop. The African's shop will shut down because he believed he was immortal and therefore saw no need to teach his children as in his illusion he saw himself always around.

Chika Onyeani's spider web economic doctrine must be taken very seriously by us Africans if we are to reverse our economic situation and tragedy. We need to get it in our heads that development will not come from aid. Aid, if it is of the right type, will only help to create the foundation upon which wealth may be created. The way to create wealth is through trade or investment.

Currently in much of Africa, Africans are employees while Indians and Chinese own the shops and businesses. The Africans spend their hard earned money patronizing these shops and businesses. The businesses, however, rarely invest back to the African communities. According to Chika Onyeani, when one invests a dollar to a community it immediately translates into 8 dollars and shortly after through the multiplier effect it becomes 164 dollars! We, the Africans are therefore sponsoring the prosperity of the other groups who sometimes instead of thanking us, pay us back with insults.

I went to buy some car part from an Indian shop the other day. While I was inside the shop, an assistant came to tell the owner of the shop that some customers were outside and they wanted to buy a second hand car which was on display. The owner went out of the shop, took a look at the two young men who had come to buy the car and without giving them a chance to speak, chased them away because he said they did not look like they could afford the car. Why in the world would I still want to do business with such a man? Unfortunately, that is exactly what the majority of us still do. When other people insult us, our parents, and our women we pay them back with more patronage. Working conditions of our people working in their establishments are among the worst in the world and we still sponsor their prosperity.

It is very important that we establish parallel businesses to those of other groups and raise our standards to compete favorably. We need to learn to work together. We need to pool our resources together and set up parallel businesses. Then we need to patronize our brothers' and sisters' businesses because by patronizing these businesses we are investing in ourselves. Buying African should be the motto of every African who is concerned about the sad economic situation of the continent. Being easy to do business with should be the motto of all African-owned businesses.

Conclusion

Positioning Africa is about strategy. The essence of strategy is competitive advantage. Without competition there would be no need for strategy. It is about knowing oneself and knowing the enemy. It is about maximizing one's assets in exploiting the competitor's weaknesses. The purpose of strategic planning therefore is to enable the concerned entity to gain, as efficiently as possible, a sustainable edge over its competitors. Africa finds herself in the position of the underdog. In such a situation, it is almost impossible to win against the giants in direct competition. Strategy in that situation means doing something different and fighting in different battlegrounds. Ohmae (1982: 237) advises that the way to compete against established giants is to avoid doing the same things as they are doing and in their familiar battleground. This is the way that Asians have managed to compete against Western countries and companies despite their large markets and greater cumulative experience in technology, production and marketing. He emphasizes the point by stating, "Choosing the battleground so that they would not have to fight head on against large Western enterprises has been the key to the success of Japanese corporations. They have sought out markets, functions and product ranges where they could initially avoid head to head competition. As a result, the Japanese production style, design and engineering approaches and personnel management philosophies are so different today that Western companies find it extremely difficult to fight back or catch up with their Japanese competitors" (Ohmae, 1982: 241).

The answer for Africa is not to do it as the Japanese or Chinese or whoever does it. It is in understanding the principles behind their strategies in order to formulate our own locally relevant strategies. To be effective, however, the strategies for positioning Africa in the globalized world for economic independence, the following prerequisites are critical:

- The first priority in positioning Africa is modernizing agriculture. Economic independence is not possible without investing in the agriculture sector. The impact of agricultural growth in a developing country on poverty reduction is four times that of other sectors (Amoako, 2008: 6). Agriculture has mostly been neglected by many governments and organizations on the continent resulting in Africa being a net importer of food. Key areas of focus in achieving modernization of agriculture include: improving productivity of labor, investing in use of appropriate technology like use of organic manure, storage etc, finding institutional solutions to the challenges that small holder farmers face in an increasingly commercialized and globalized agricultural economy and to shift from exporting raw materials to processed products.

Promoting the efficiency of agricultural markets will play a key role in this. According to Poole (2008:10 – 11), promoting efficient markets will include: organization, understanding, specialization, co-ordination and partnership.

Farmers and traders need to organize themselves. The decisions of individual farmers and traders are too small to make a difference. The farmers and traders need to understand and respect each others' role in the chain and concentrate on their specific roles for efficiency and synergy. Coordination will help farmers to produce what consumers want and the traders to deliver the inputs and credit that the farmers need. Partnership helps to develop a shared vision and a joint plan to identify new market opportunities and overcome problems together like lobbying the local government for better roads and market stalls and for provision of electricity for developing processing businesses.

It is not wise to fight giants in their familiar grounds because *it was ignorance that made the mouse to challenge the cat to the wrestling match.* Just Change – a network of poor farmers in India is showing a way to change the fighting ground and avoid fighting giants head on and benefit rather than being harmed from the global market or globalization. Just Change connects poor farmers in India who produce and process tea and other produce which they export to poor communities in the UK who still offer better margins than the multinational companies or the other normal marketing channels. Just Change connects with the Marsh Farm group, a group of 3000 people living on a housing estate near Luton, in Southern England (Thekaekara, 2008: 23).

In addition to improvement in agriculture for local consumption and export, there is a need to shift towards manufacturing and services in areas that will not involve a head-to-head competition with cheaper imports from other more developed countries. Government intervention to protect local manufactures and service providers is indispensable.

- African governments need to invest in infrastructure at national, regional and continental levels to enable Africa to participate effectively in the globalized world. This is purely a matter of leadership. I live in a country where we had a government that for 10 years managed to almost convince us that development in general and construction of the above infrastructure in our country was impossible. The next government came and reversed the situation within 3 years with construction of considerable infrastructure and general economic improvement. I am afraid to say part of the economic struggle for economic liberation of the continent will involve fighting tooth and nail political leaders standing in the way of our economic freedom. If our leaders or governments do not create an enabling environment, they do not deserve to be in office and we must be men enough to remove them.

We have always blamed leaders but we need to blame the followers too. I was very surprised to discover that there are people who do not like good leaders. They do not like leaders who treat them with respect and as adults. They despise such leaders as weak. They would rather be led by dictators. In fact they prefer to be led by dictators.

In one country I heard young professionals saying they would really want to see regime change but not with person who was leading the campaign for change because they said he was not 'as strong as the dictator they were trying to remove'. In other words, they were saying they would rather have the dictator than this person. There are employees who will interpret good and empowering leadership as weakness. They want supervisors who literary shout at them. They want leaders who when they see they should run away from. They want leaders who when they call them to their offices they should literally tremble. They want leaders they can fear rather than respect. I am really baffled by this phenomenon and maybe my learned psychologist friends can explain it to me. Then there are those who will respect and show all the loyalty to leaders or supervisors who are of other races and not their fellow Africans. I really struggle to understand this. Through these actions we create the dictators ourselves and then complain that we have a monster.

Investing in infrastructure makes regional integration possible. Regional integration creates larger markets and improves the mobility of goods and services. Today, it costs more to ship a ton of wheat from Kenya to neighboring Uganda than it does to ship it across the Atlantic.

- Knowledge creation for solving the continent's economic problems and entrepreneurship are the two levers that will lift Africa out of her economic slavery. Education must be education for economic empowerment. It is very surprising to see African graduates working for Indians and Chinese who are far less qualified than them on types of work where the Africans by virtue of their education should be leaders. This puts the value of such an education into question. The divide in the world now is between those with wealth-creating knowledge and those who do not. The Indians and Chinese, for example, have wealth-creating knowledge. Africa must learn to be part of the knowledge based world – knowledge for wealth creation. Knowledge for wealth creation must, among other things, contribute towards addressing the problem of unemployment. About 70 percent of young people in Ethiopia, for example, are unemployed. In Nigeria, with a population of about 150 million people, the problem is more acute. Wealth-creating knowledge must help in creating creative and innovative small and medium enterprises to keep the young people meaningfully employed. In high income countries, the Small and Medium Enterprises (SME) sector has been estimated to contribute more than 50% of the gross GDP and it is the engine of new job creation and source of as much as half of the innovation of these economies. In Africa, the contribution to GDP of the SMEs has been estimated at 10% (Amoako, 2008: 11).

- There is need for cultural restoration. We need once more to consciously embrace our ubuntu culture and take it beyond its social value to its yet to be realized economic value. We need to patronize each other's businesses. Buy African must be our motto. Being easy to do business with must be the motto of all African businesses.

Like there were political founding fathers, there is a need for another era for economic founding fathers. It is important to emphasize at this point that while globalization offers potential for great opportunities, as long as the playing field is not leveled there will not be much hope for Africa to thrive and start on the road to utopia. The playing ground today is seriously skewed against the developing countries and Africa in general. To quote Castro (2007: 308) again,

There is no capitalism today. There is no competition. Today what we have are monopolies in all the great sectors. There is some competition between certain countries to produce televisions or computers but capitalism does not exist anymore.

Five hundred global corporations today control 80% of the world's economy. Prices don't stem from competition. The prices at which for example medicines to fight AIDS are sold are monopolistic. Medicines continue to be one of the most abusive, extravagant and exploitative items in the world's budgets...Advertizing determines what sells and what does not. The person who doesn't have much money cannot advertize his products in any way even if they are excellent.

This is where the efforts of international civil society come to play. Globalization without justice, values and consideration of the stages of development of the 'where African countries are' will only continue to push the continent towards its oblivion.

Donors will need to play a role in the struggle for Africa's economic independence. Artulo Escobar (1997: 86) writes:

The organizing premise was the belief in the role of modernization...This view determined the belief that capital investment was the most important ingredient in economic growth and development. The advance of poor countries was thus seen from the outset as depending on ample supplies of capital to provide for infrastructure, industrialization, and the overall modernization of society. Where was this capital to come from? One possible answer was domestic savings. But because these countries were seen as trapped in a 'vicious cycle' of poverty and lack of capital, so that a good part of the 'badly needed' capital would have to come from abroad...Moreover, it is absolutely necessary that governments and international organizations take an active role in promoting and orchestrating the necessary efforts to overcome general backwardness and economic underdevelopment.

In summary, Thabo Mbeki agrees with Artulo Escobar when he comments on the above quotation by observing:

> First, as has been the case throughout human history, capital investment is central to Africa's economic growth and development. Secondly, Africa requires ample supplies of capital to provide for infrastructure, industrialization, and overall modernization of society. Thirdly, one source of capital is domestic savings. Fourth, most of our countries are trapped in a vicious cycle of poverty and lack of capital. Fifth, a good part of the required capital must therefore come from abroad. Lastly, donors have to play an active role in Africa's necessary efforts to overcome general backwardness and economic underdevelopment (Mbeki, 2001: 188).

Just like *a mother of twins must sleep on her back* so that she can serve or breast feed her babies more conveniently, Africa must reposition herself through self effort and the help of international civil society and donors for more significance in the world.

CHAPTER 9: WHAT WOULD AN ECONOMICALLY LIBERATED AFRICA LOOK LIKE?

Introduction

What is development? What is the difference between the developed countries and the not developed countries? When the not developed countries, which is what all the countries in Africa are, become developed are they going to look like the developed countries? Is that what we want? Definitely there are a lot of things we admire in the developed countries. There are also things that we do not. Even though Africa is not economically liberated, there are things we like about ourselves that we would want to preserve even when we become economically independent. In fact the ability to preserve our identity as Africans in a rapidly changing environment will be a mark of our genuine independence. It is important to paint a clear picture of what a liberated Africa would look like because *what the eyes have seen, the heart cannot forget.* In other words, the way to get heart commitment for mobilization for the struggle for the continent's economic independence is by communicating and entrenching a strong enough vision that people can buy into. It is also important to have that vision because *the person who does not know where they are going will not know whether they have arrived or not.*

Millennium Development Goals and Economic Development

The current vision driving development efforts on the continent and other developing regions today is based on the Millenium Development Goals (MDGs) summarized below:

A summary of the Millennium Development Goals

Goal 1: Eradicate extreme poverty and hunger
Goal 2: Achieve universal primary education
Goal 3: Promote gender equality and empower women
Goal 4: Reduce child mortality
Goal 5: Improve maternal health
Goal 6: Combat HIV and AIDS, malaria and other diseases
Goal 7: Ensure environmental sustainability
Goal 8: Develop global partnerships for development

Source: UNDP website (www.undp.org/mdg/goalsandindicators.html), 2006.

Personal development is a personal responsibility. Community development is the particular community's responsibility. National development is a national responsibility. Similarly continental development is a continental responsibility. No person can develop another. No country can develop another. No continent can develop another. Others can only assist or hinder. *The sympathizer cannot mourn more than the bereaved.* This is why I believe, for example, that the MDGs summarized above, while very well intended, will not go very far in helping poor people in Africa because there is no clear mechanism to make their realization a personal and community responsibility.

In addition to being biased towards social goals rather than economic growth, thereby underemphasizing the importance of economic growth (Masset and White, 2004: 279) that this book is arguing for, MDGs have largely been made governments and NGOs responsibility. I wonder how many people poor people in African rural communities today know what MDGs are and their responsibility in making the MDGs a reality. In the end all this means governments and NGOs taking the responsibility on behalf of the communities and individuals to achieve the MDGs.

An alternative to MDGs

I would want to present my vision of what an economically independent Africa would look like. Instead of presenting a grand vision for the continent, I will present my vision of an ideal African community. I will present my vision of an ideal African community because that is where the common person for whom this book is meant lives. And that is where the effectiveness of all change efforts is finally measured and that is where success or failure of such changes is most and realistically visible. This presents a personal and community responsibility perspective. It also presents a balance between economic and social development aspirations. When a critical number of communities on the continent changes, the country changes and eventually the continent will change.

We need a concise, vivid, bright, inspiring and uplifting vision of the community we are trying to create. Without this picture we have no target. Without a target you cannot hit one. As a development worker I have observed that we rarely talk about establishing an ideal picture to engage people's aspirations and unleash their potential.

The ideal African community

The ideal African community is one that represents total freedom. It represents economic, political, technological, cultural and spiritual freedom. It is to these facets that we now turn.

The economy of the ideal African community

There is enough food for every household in the community throughout the year. The food is not enough in quantity only but also in quality or nutritional value. The people are able to produce the food themselves or they can afford to buy. There is a health center with adequate and qualified personnel. When people go to the health center, they are helped because medicine is available. Because there is adequate personnel, the people do not have to spend the whole day in a queue only to be told to come again the next day because the doctor could not see them today because there were too many people in the queue.

There is an ambulance at the health center and it is in a running condition and it does not get grounded because the health center's fuel budget line has been exhausted in the first quarter of the year. Serious cases are referred to appropriate hospitals and the ambulance is there to take the people to the hospital without fail.

The community has good all-weather roads. The community is therefore connected to the country's road network. Young people from the community staying in town or outside the country do not have to think twice before visiting parents and relatives in the community because they wonder whether their cars will reach their homes and if they can, whether their cars will be able to drive out of the communities due to the poor condition of the roads. The ambulance can comfortably take patients to the hospital without further hurting the patients because of the bumps on the road.

The members of the community have good huts or houses. The most important thing about those houses is that they have enough space for all the people who are living in them. They are well ventilated. They do not leak when it rains. People sleep on a bed and not on a reed mat. They have comfortable mattresses and adequate covering.

The people can afford good clothes. They do not rely for their clothing on second hand clothes thrown away in Europe and America. They can afford brand new clothes. Everyone can afford shoes. No one is walking barefoot except by choice not by financial constraint. No one in the community therefore has cracked feet.

Every child in the community is going to school. At least primary school is compulsory. Every parent understands the importance of education and no one has to coerce parents to send their children to school because the importance of school is obvious to everyone in the community. The schools have adequate modern class rooms with adequate facilities. The children are not learning under a tree anymore. There are adequate and improved water and sanitation facilities at each school. The pupil-teacher ratio is the internationally accepted one. There is gender balance among the teachers and among the pupils. The parents and teachers are working together as partners in management of the schools and in the teaching of the children. The schools are within reach so that children do not have to wait another five years to be old enough to walk the long distances to school. The streets to and from the schools are safe for the children.

The community has a modern shopping center where all the basic commodities can be found at prices not so different from town or city centers. The most important thing is that the shopping center is owned by the community members and not by outsiders. Each community is producing products and services and there are ready and profitable markets locally and internationally for the products and services. The community is working as a cooperative to effect economies of scale and ensure synergy and to also increase its bargaining power. Exploitative middle men have been cut out.

The community has a bank or at least a bank agency in which every member of the community has a savings account. Everyone in the community can read, write and count and therefore can participate meaningfully in community life.

In short, the people in the community have control over their resources and they are turning these resources into wealth. The people, especially the youths are gainfully employed. Every one is productive according to the age and ability.

No one is idle. The community is attractive enough to prevent youths from unnecessary emigration.

The politics of an ideal African community

The leaders are democratically elected. They are elected to the satisfaction of both the winners and losers. There is no rigging. The leaders are elected based on merit rather than party and tribal loyalty. The leaders are servants of the people. They represent the will and the values of the people. The leaders are elected from among the people. They stay in the community together with the people. They do not stay in town and only show up during elections. The leaders are held accountable. They account for their decisions and actions. The people can make legitimate claims and demands on the leaders and the leaders listen and respond. In general the community takes a questioning stance. Elections are free and fair. Presidents are not sworn in while votes are still being counted. Enough time is given between announcing results and swearing in ceremonies to give confidence that their victory is genuine and to ensure smooth and realistic transitions from the incumbent president to the president elect.

Diversity is embraced rather than taken as a source of division and strife. Conflicts are seen as opportunity for growth and better understanding of each other. The leaders are respected rather than feared.

There is security for everyone. People can sleep at night with their doors open. There is no fear. There is a police station and justice is meted to criminals. No one is above the law.

The technology of an ideal African community

The community has telephone services. The phones actually work and are affordable. It does not cost one the moon to make a simple phone call. There is an internet center in the community. It is possible to browse the internet; send and receive e-mails at reasonable prices. They are able to connect with the rest of the world for business opportunities and transactions through the internet. There is a resource center or library which stocks relevant materials – information and knowledge that can help the community members turn their resources into wealth. Each household has a radio or TV set and they are able to access local and international content.

Every household has access to electricity. People do not have to cut down trees and destroy the environment for fuel anymore.

There are efficient, affordable and safe transport systems to and fro the community. People are using more efficient and effective tools for farming and raising their livestock. There is less dependence on high cost inorganic inputs. Farming inputs are available.

Every household has access to safe and clean water. Every household has access to improved sanitation and sewerage systems. Surroundings are clean and hygienic. Waste is disposed hygienically.

The culture of an economically liberated African community

The principle feature of the community is that people and relationships are more important than things, there is sharing of collective ownership of opportunities, responsibilities and challenges. There is participatory decision making and leadership, loyalty and patriotism, and reconciliation as a goal of conflict management.

There is a playground for the children. Children are valued. They are actively and visibly involved in community decisions and activities. The role of elderly members of the community as custodians of culture and wisdom is restored. Elderly people are respected and consulted for their wisdom. Parenting is once again a collective responsibility.

There is a community meeting center where members of the community occasionally meet to discuss issues facing the community. There is unity and such meetings are seen as a way of strengthening the unity. The culture of community festivals is restored. No one is too busy for such events. Members from other communities are invited and they make contributions in dances, games, folklore, etc. The cultural shows at such events foster unity by celebrating diversity. The community is embracing a reading culture. They are learning from their experience and they are documenting their lessons for themselves and the future generations.

People are open to positive external culture and are embracing change. They are preserving those cultural aspects that are useful and relevant and discarding those that have become obsolete. They are proud of their identity.

The people command respect because of their character and dignity. External agencies working in the community listen to the people. The activities of these agencies complement rather than replace the people's efforts for self-development.

The ideal community is well summarized by Gandhi when he says, "When our villages are fully developed there will be no dearth in them of men and women with a high degree of skill and artistic talent. There will be village poets, village artists, village architects, linguists and research workers. In short there will be nothing in life worthy having which will not be had in the villages. Today the villages are dung heaps. Tomorrow they will be like tiny gardens of Eden where dwell intelligent folk whom no one can deceive or exploit" (Sachs, 1980: 49)

Conclusion

The economically liberated African community is one in which people are free. They are free economically, socio-culturally, technologically and spiritually. They can therefore exert economic, political, socio-cultural and spiritual influence on the nation and the continent. In short, a process of genuine development must result in:

- More physically, mentally and spiritually healthy individuals and communities
- Job creation and better jobs for people
- More disposable income for individuals and their families

- Strong and healthy families and marriages capable of raising their children to live better lives than their parents did.

Given the continental resource endowment we have, we deserved this community yesterday – not tomorrow. It is a catching up game. Let the conscious struggle begin with every man, woman, boy, girl at individual, family, community, organizational, national and continental level to take personal and collective responsibility.

In terms of organization, this will mean that the communities and organizations serving them will have to become 'sovereign communities' – a term I was introduced to by Doug Reeler of Community Development Association (CDRA) South Africa. Sovereign communities and organizations are those that:

- Work with their own purposes and values
- Express the will and voice of own constituencies
- Are culturally and structurally unique
- Serve their own agenda in meeting the needs of the people they serve and not that of donors
- Are politically conscious and ask their own questions
- Are able to learn and adapt from own experience
- Are able to cooperate and collaborate

In short, they promote and enable the individuals and communities they serve to become self-reliant, ensure local ownership and make own decisions. In all the countries that have managed to transform themselves economically and socially, the key ingredients to success have been a responsive government, socially friendly economic policies and a universal provisioning of social services. The business or entrepreneurial sector is responsible for generating economic growth. The government is responsible for social development while civil society is responsible for holding both the government and the business sectors accountable in fulfilling their obligations to the people they exist for (Mehrotra and Jolly, 1998: 432).

CHAPTER 10: THE FIVE STEP STRATEGY FOR AFRICA'S ECONOMIC INDEPENDENCE

Introduction

Inspired by the discussion held by a group of young professional Africans from different countries at a hotel in Antananarivo, Madagascar, the book set out to identify and explore the topmost African problem. Using the strategic fit model and drawing on lessons from other countries that have transformed themselves economically like South Korea, Singapore and China, the problem was identified as Africa's failure to transform its resources into wealth. Ways to address this fundamental problem were explored through reflecting on the following strategic questions:

- What is development and what would a 'developed' Africa look like?
- Why have past and current efforts to develop Africa failed?
- What should Africa's topmost economic development priority be?
- Who should lead Africa's effort to economically catch up with the rest of the world?
- How can Africa break the aid dependence?
- Which other countries or regions have developed in the recent past? How did they do it? What can we learn from them?

Africa's topmost economic development priority

Simply put, development is good change. It is sustainable improvement in people's lives. It is freedom. An economically liberated African community is one in which people are free. They are free economically, socio-culturally, technologically and spiritually. They can therefore exert economic, political, socio-cultural and spiritual influence on the nation and the continent. Development must enable people to enjoy their world.

The book has shown that past and current development efforts have failed because they are based on aid as an end in itself and not as a means for capital to create wealth. In short past development efforts have failed because they were not based on wealth creation. They concentrated on wealth distribution by governments and NGOs or CSOs. In the three centers of power: the state, the economy (businesses) and the civil society, this has meant the state, as a recipient of donor money, being more powerful than the other two. For development to happen there is need for a balance of power among the three. In Africa the state is often more powerful than the other two; as a result there are inadequate checks and balances on the state, leading to corruption.

Since the state does not create wealth but only distributes the money received from donors, there is no sustainable wealth creation as the business sector or economy is usually weak. A bigger challenge is that of the few businesses (small and big) on the continent, most do not belong to the locals. They belong to foreigners who usually transfer all the profits to their countries of origin.

Africa's topmost economic development priority is to create its own wealth and reduce dependence on non-developmental donor aid. Wealth is raw materials or energy compounded by intellect's know-how (Buckminister Fuller, 1969: 241). Africa has an abundance of natural resources (fossil fuels, coal, oil etc) and power like tidal waves, water, the wind, gravity, the sun, etc. What the continent has failed to do is to organize its 'intellect's know-how" to compound these resources into wealth. Africa's topmost economic development priority therefore is to organize its 'intellect's know-how' to create wealth. It is to invest in an enabling environment for inventions and innovations. It is also to invest in the ability to use the already existing innovations and inventions that others are already using in creating wealth.

For a long time in Africa, development has been led by the state. At some point there was a shift to make development civil society led. There is a conversion now back to state-led development. But the state does not create wealth, it only distributes it. Civil society does not distribute wealth; when effective, all it can do is hold power holders accountable. Business people are profit oriented and their interest in people is their profit motive.

Logically therefore, economic leadership based on inventions and innovations can only be taken neither by the government, or civil society or businesses. Students mostly at university levels are much better suited to take this role (Buckminister Fuller, 1969: 291). There is need, therefore, to promote and organize the institutions of higher learning and research centers and other innovators and inventors into a fourth center of power (in addition to the state, the civil society and business). There is a need on the continent for a pool of educated, intelligent young people armed with the technical know-how of America, Europe and Japan to lead in the economic catching up game of transforming Africa's resources into wealth like it has been done in China, India, Singapore and South Korea. The young people in diaspora can and should make an important contribution to this effort.

The wealth thus created would eventually offer an alternative to non-developmental aid and a complement to developmental aid which Africa still needs to out-grow from some day, the sooner the better. This is not to say that we do not need aid. But for aid to be truly developmental, it must be seen as a transition measure with a clear end in sight. For aid to be truly developmental, it must contribute towards wealth creation on the continent and for the continent and not only distribution through the state or civil society organizations. The nature of the aid debate needs to move beyond better quantity and quality aid to include aid supporting the creation of own wealth for the continent.

The central message of the book is that for Africa to develop, there is need to re-orient the public from prime dependence on politics and the aid system to organizing innovation and invention for wealth creation.

The challenge to Africa's young people

Africa remains the greatest developmental challenge in the world today and in the foreseeable future. Others can help or hinder Africa's development but the responsibility for the economic future of Africa lies with the Africans themselves on the continent and in the diaspora. The challenge is particularly pointed to young people as in the words of the Japanese Prime minister, Junichiro Kuizumi:

"In any age, it is always the young people with the spirit of self help and self-discipline, concern for others, and a high aspiration who pioneer a new era. It is people who are the engine for reform" (Chikago, 2003: 1).

Today the young people of China and India are the most optimistic people in the world. They feel and believe that the future belongs to them. It is this optimism and energy that is fueling the economic momentum of these two countries. They are ambitious and are geared to make their mark and change the world. Martin Luther King Jr. advised, "We must constantly stimulate our youth to rise above the stagnant level of mediocrity and seek to achieve excellence in their various fields of endeavor. Doors are opening now that were not open in the past, and the great challenge is to be ready to enter these doors as they open. No greater tragedy could befall us at this hour but that of allowing new opportunities to emerge without concomitant preparedness to meet them" (Washington, 1991: 151).

Most of us Africans get satisfied too soon with too little. The dream of most young men is to finish school, get a good job, have a company car, marry a beautiful girl, have children and live in a good house provided by the company. That is selfish thinking. There is a great need to think bigger. There is need to think about one's contribution to the economic liberation of the communities, countries and the continent. That is real success. Africa is still waiting for her African economic liberators. Is this the generation that will bring about that liberation or Africa still has to wait for another? The current parents have failed their children. Will today's young people fail their children as well?

The foregoing has serious implications for education and the curricula in Africa. Much of Africa's education does not equip the young people with questioning or critical skills. It is not enough to teach the children that the sun rises in the east and sets in the west. They must be taught like the children in the West and East why it is that the sun rises in the east and sets in the west as well. It is this questioning stance that creates momentum for personal and collective change. There is need for a curriculum that would promote creativity and self reliance and a strong foundation for innovation and inventions. In the words of a reverend, William Murray, *what you want to see in a country, first put it in schools.*

Related to more relevant curricula is the need for practical use of knowledge gained. My own life took an upward turn at the age of 28 when I came across Napoleon Hill's book, *Think and Grow Rich.* I read the book at least a 100 times until one day 'my eyes were opened and for the first time I caught the vision of the author'. This was a turning point for me and I began to immediately order my life according to the message and principles in the book. The turning point helped me to find my place in the war for Africa's economic independence. In short, it turned me into an economic warrior for the continent and myself. Young people have a challenge to get knowledge and then make practical use of that knowledge. The problem today is that many of us have a genius in not making practical use of the knowledge we have. The difference between successful people and failures is the knowledge these people have, the relevance of that knowledge and whether that knowledge is put to practical use or not.

It is not my intention in this book to discuss the subject of self-development but let it suffice to say that academic qualifications on their own are inadequate to bring out an individual's full potential. In fact, the failure to use in practical terms knowledge acquired is linked to lack of conscious self-development initiative in the individual. Every young person who is serious about using their life for a worthwhile cause like economic independence of their country and the continent need to work out a plan for self-development besides whatever academic or professional qualifications they have (Canfield, 2007: 21).

A challenge for young people on the continent is to put their respect for their parents in perspective. As Mansfield (2005: 263) notes, "Every new generation must be very careful about what it accepts from its parents' time. It is true that we want to receive good from those who have come before us, but we must also understand the difference between living truth and ensnaring tradition". Our parents and most of their traditions have failed to bring about economic independence for the continent. They have failed to recognize that, man has found that he is endowed with a powerful brain which has found out what a few of the invisible principles operative in the physical environment can do. And that the universe having permitted him to discover his and her intellectual effectiveness as well as some of the universe's riches, and thus to participate consciously as well as sub-consciously in universal evolution, will now require him to use his intellect directly and effectively thus making success or failure humanity's responsibility (Buckminister Fuller, 1969: 290 – 291).

The challenge for young people on the continent is to rise up and be counted in the struggle for the economic independence of the continent through the use of the intellect as wealth which is the basis of economic independence is 'natural resources compounded by intellect's know-how'.

The enemy is us

Africa has undergone two major changes. The first was the political independence wave from the colonial masters. The second wave was for democratic change – introducing multiparty democracy. This time around there is need for a continent wide revolution for economic independence. This will take nothing short of a revolution in thinking and practice. In the struggle for political independence the enemy was clear. It was the colonial master. In the battle for multiparty democracy the enemy was the dictators. In the struggle for economic independence, the enemy is much stronger and subtle because the enemy is in each one of us as Africans.

To conquer self is the most formidable task in the world. It is the ultimate test of responsibility. *By climbing the mountain we do not conquer the mountain but ourselves.* By climbing the mountain of African economic slavery we are 'conquering' ourselves to gain true victory and independence because we are our own enemy. Conquering self means changing our mindset from dependence to independence and ultimately to interdependence.

The clue to winning the struggle for the economic independence of Africa is for Africans to begin owning assets and businesses small and large and patronizing one another. It is a catching up game. There is a need to catch up with the others in assets, investments and business ownership. It must be the goal to balance or set up parallel businesses owned by others on the continent and eventually to take over no matter what or how long it takes. *A journey of a thousand miles starts with one step.* This is a struggle that will require more intensity than the struggle for political independence which is really meaningless without economic independence. The greatest secret in the world is that one's external environment reflects one's internal environment or condition. Africa's economic, political, technological and socio-cultural situation reflects the collective African mindset. The struggle for Africa's economic independence is about awakening and changing this mindset.

State level interventions

State level interventions to turn around the African situation are amply documented and summarized below by Calderisi (2007: 207 – 222):

- *Introduce mechanisms for tracing and recovering public funds*
  Billions of dollars stolen by people like Sani Abacha and Mobutu Seseseko have been lost to European banks because there are no effective ways to trace such money. Such loop holes create opportunities for corrupted leaders to divert state funds to personal accounts. It is encouraging that in some NGOs or non profit organizations people are now being dragged to court or at least be made to account for misuse of donor money. A few countries on the continent have anti-corruption bureaus that would take on this responsibility. But unfortunately many of the anti-corruption bureaus are just toothless bulldogs proving the unfortunate proverb, *the law is like cobwebs, only small insects get caught in it.*

- *Require all heads of state, ministers, MPs and senior officials to open their bank accounts to public scrutiny*
  The refusal by many presidents, ministers, MPs and senior officials to declare their assets and open their bank accounts to public scrutiny is evidence enough that they have something to hide. And indeed, the 'economic transformation' of these people once they get into power is amazing and often their decline after losing elections, for example, is equally amazing.

- *Cut direct aid to individual countries in half*
  Calderisi (2007: 209) argues that abundant aid is bad for African countries because it offers false hope, dampens initiative to develop the continent's own resources, including its people. Aid must always be an add-on to what the country already has and not a substitute.

- *Focus   direct aid on four or five countries that are serious about reducing poverty*
  The point on this one is that only those countries that show seriousness on poverty reduction based on agreed indicators should be taken seriously in aid considerations. This would act as a motivation to the less serious countries to change. Mr Calderesi suggests five countries that should be given such treatment. I am not willing to commend any country because my experience traveling to different countries on the continent and some of the ones that he mentions is that the situation on the ground may not always reflect what official documents say.

- *Require all countries to hold internationally supervised elections*
  The 2008 elections in Kenya and Zimbabwe are a shame to Africa and have set a very bad precedent. In fact what the elections have managed to demonstrate is that presidents in power can lose elections and decide to go nowhere. What this trend says is that it is no longer important to win or lose elections as winners and losers rule together in the so-called power-sharing arrangements. Aid tied to free and fair elections would discourage some of these behaviors.

- *Promote other aspects of democracy including a free press and an independent judiciary*
  One would expect that opposition parties would vehemently fight for a free press and an independent judiciary. One observes, however, that they are not keen because they know that when they win and go into power, they will behave just the same and they do not want to put unnecessary strings around their necks.

- *Supervise the running of Africa's schools and HIV and AIDS programs*
  This means improving the quality of the now famous free primary education. Quantity from the free primary education has undermined the quality of education in many countries. A few countries including Uganda had their AIDS Support money through the National AIDS Commissions suspended because of allegations of abuse. Uganda may not be an exception on this.

- *Establish citizen review groups to oversee government policy and aid agreements*
  The primary mandate of these groups would be social accountability – holding government and other power holders accountable. One important area they would focus on is on how debt relief resources are being used. In many countries I have traveled, local citizens wonder what difference debt relief has made to their lives. Parliamentarians in many African countries hold so much power that the citizens have no influence on them at all. In Malawi, parliamentarians decided not to pass the national budget and there wasn't much ordinary citizens would do about it. These groups therefore would play a critical role in balancing the power of such power holders.

- *Put more emphasis on infrastructure and regional links*
  Today, Africa is left out of the globalized world because it does not have the infrastructure that effective participation in globalization requires. There isn't much aid invested in roads, ports, railways, airports, water, power and telecommunication facilities. Without this physical connection facilities, any talk of economic development becomes just a joke. Western donors are very reluctant to make this type of investment as they prefer social rather than economic development. China's investment in Africa may put pressure on Western donors to make serious efforts in infrastructure investment (Lonnqvist, 2008: 10).

- *Merge the World Bank, IMF and UNDP*
  The World Bank, IMF and UNDP could create synergy if they harmonized their missions by merging into one institution. The World Bank focuses on long term health of economies. IMF's focus is short-term. UNDP focuses on supporting capacity building. All these three would be better done under one institution. Africa being the greatest developmental challenge in the world would become the central focus of the new merged institution. The merger would also make the institution more efficient by reducing administrative costs that can be redirected to programs. Sachs (2005: 366) observes that the three institutions have the experience and technical sophistication to play an important role. They have the motivation of a highly professional staff. Yet, they have been, especially the World Bank and the IMF, badly used, as creditor run agencies rather than international institutions representing all of their 182 member governments. The foregoing measures would help restore the international role of these institutions to once again become champions of economic justice and helpers rather than a hindrance to Africa' economic independence.

In short, the above measures are calling for the need for a developmental state which according to Amoako (2008: 12) must focus on: demonstrating good leadership and governance by setting a clear vision and executing the development strategy effectively, ensuring macro-economic stability, understanding our assets, growth engines and comparative advantages or what makes sense for our economy in the context of global trends; and finally allowing markets to allocate resources while protecting vulnerable individuals and groups.

The above measures would create an enabling environment for wealth creation in Africa. The measures are very important but they are not sufficient for wealth creation and therefore economic development for Africa. This is because the state does not produce wealth. It only distributes wealth that has already been created somewhere. This book goes beyond these recommendations to suggest a way Africa can liberate herself through own wealth creation as learnt from observation and from those countries or regions that have lifted themselves from economic slavery.

Africa remains the greatest developmental challenge in the world. In order to move forward, it is naïve to think that African problems are caused by the West and that African problems must be solved by Africans only or that African problems should have African solutions only. At the same time, I am a strong believer that *the sympathizer cannot mourn more than the bereaved* which means that Africans themselves should take leadership is solving their problems. The recommendations that follow demonstrate how Africans themselves can demonstrate leadership in solving their economic development challenge.

The five step strategy for Africa's economic liberation
In this book I have proposed a five step strategy to employ in the struggle for the economic liberation and independence of Africa. The strategy focuses on what young people especially students supported by civil society organizations can do. This is my humble contribution and my hope is that others may build on this to come up with a more refined strategy. One more time the strategy is summarized below:

Acknowledging that Africa is not economically independent
The first step in the struggle for the economic liberation of Africa is to acknowledge that Africa is not economically independent yet and that this is the most formidable challenge facing the continent today. Most other challenges on the continent are just symptoms of this fundamental challenge. This fact is supposed to inflame us with constructive anger to take constructive and corrective action. If one does not have capacity for constructive anger that can drive them to action, I suggest they read Chika Onyeani's *Capitalist Nigger* to get inflamed by the sad state of the black race in general and the African people in particular. If that cannot move them, then I am afraid to say they are not fit to be enlisted as a soldier in this struggle.

Africa is not economically independent because it has failed to transform its resources into wealth. Africa has the largest natural and mineral resource endowment but it is home to the poorest people on earth because it has failed to transform these resources into wealth. It was the realization that economic development is the country's or continent's own responsibility and that in waiting for others to develop us, we will wait for ever that got country's like South Korea and Singapore, for example, on their path to economic independence and success.

Creating visions of aspiration
South Korea was fortunate to have visionary leaders who were able to see an economically transformed country if only they found the right strategy that they did in Sun Tzu's book, *The Art of War*. With this they were able to communicate or even force their vision on the country until it became a reality. In Africa, Botswana is an example of a country where visions of aspiration are used effectively to focus community and national energy towards achieving agreed national goals and targets. Based on chapter 9 (what would an economically liberated African community look like?) the young people and

everyone on the continent in general must be helped to create an ideal picture of an economically independent or an economically free community. They must believe and believe for real that the realization of the ideal community is possible. They must be convinced beyond any shadow of doubt that they and the people in communities deserve the life they have described for themselves in their ideal pictures. Most importantly, they must know that the weapons for fighting in the struggle for economic liberation are not the conventional weapons of machetes and guns but knowledge and brain power.

Organizing for wealth creation

Africa's greatest need is organizing for wealth-creating knowledge and its application. This is organizing for economic power. This is how countries like the United States, Ireland, China and South Korea have managed to gain leadership in the globalized world. Organizing for wealth-creation knowledge will enable the Africans to know the resources they have, their value and how to transform them into their wealth. Because they do not have this knowledge, those who have it have taken control of their resources and they are creating wealth out of them. The greatest weapon in wealth creation is knowledge and brain power. Education, therefore, must be for creation of knowledge and development of brain power for solving the continent's real challenges, the number one of which is its economic liberation. There is need to discard all filler materials in the curricula and concentrate on this most important challenge. Knowledge that is useful is that which will enable Africans to begin to manufacture those commodities it does not make sense to import from outside. Honestly speaking, it does not make sense to import tooth picks, bottle tops, pins, pens, buttons, treadle pumps and clothes when all the raw materials for making these products are found in abundance on the continent.

There is need for a type of organizations that would harness the innovation and invention potential on the continent. This type of organization would be what Patel (2005: 216) calls 'innovation and development valleys and hubs' the purpose of which would be to concentrate on wealth creation, maximize the chance of making breakthroughs, attracting talent and capital and creating commercial enterprises. Such organizations would be concerned with cultivating national and the continent's economic niche in the world. Such organizations would for example:

- Identify local innovations and inventions from institutions like secondary schools, technical colleges, universities and communities. Test the innovations and inventions for their relative advantage, compatibility, simplicity, triability, and observability (Rogers, 1983: 36). The innovations must promote giving everyone an opportunity to earn a decent livelihood and employing the idle labor force in the production of necessities. This is the way to refuse the colonial logic that has put Africa as a reservoir of raw materials. The innovations must enable processing the raw materials to create jobs for the youths and everyone.

- Identify, collect and contextualize relevant innovations and inventions developed elsewhere. There is no need to reinvent the wheel. Shapiro (2008: 18) notes that a society's capacity to quickly adopt and adapt innovations developed by others is at least as important economically as its capacity to come up with innovation breakthroughs itself.
- Facilitate patent rights between inventors and innovators on one hand and businesses and governments on the other
- caling up the innovations and inventions for community benefit
- Motivating and supporting the innovators and inventors, for example, through scholarships, cash and special recognition
- Lobbying donors to fund and support this initiative and convincing them that this is a more sustainable way of ensuring economic development on the continent. Support establishment of innovation-based businesses by local entrepreneurs. The new philanthropy in the likes of Bill Gates, Buffet Warren, Richard Branson and the many other billionaires and millionaires who are committing a part of their wealth to philanthropy offer a rare opportunity, complement an alternative to the official aid system. Bill Gates donates more money per year than the whole of UNICEF. If part of this money is invested in creating business and entrepreneurial power on the continent, it would make a big contribution towards the economic independence struggle.
- Raising awareness and supporting local businesses to use sophisticated management methods, information technologies, Internet based tools available to build and manage national, continental and global networks (Shapiro, 2008: 181).

On a visit to Malawi, former US President Bill Clinton said, intelligence and ability are evenly distributed on the globe. What is not evenly distributed are investment, opportunities and systems that enable people to unleash their potential. This is what the above types of organization would do – providing investment, opportunities and systems for inventors and innovators to unleash their potential.

Inventions and innovations are the way to bypass systematic resistance aimed at keeping the rich getting richer while the poor are getting poorer. This is because innovators and inventors do not need a licence to innovate or invent and if their innovations and inventions are genuine they are irresistible.

Wealth-creating knowledge must enable Africa to achieve productivity leaps. Productivity leaps for example are moving millions of people in China from 18th century agriculture to 21st century industry and commerce. There are three levels of productivity. These are arithmetic, geometric and exponential. Productivity leaps means being able to jump from arithmetic to exponential levels. There is need in Africa to develop or use ideas that can fully employ each of the millions of people on the continent so that working becomes a personal option not a privilege.

It may surprise many that while the notion of economic independence sounds naturally good, not every one is in a hurry to see an economically independent Africa. Most politicians who run governments are not. They prosper through the continued poverty of their people. Most civil society organizations do not show the urgency of the need for economic independence of the continent. It is clear most donors are not in a hurry to see an economically independent Africa soon. Businesses are interested with profit for now and not to develop local entrepreneurship and business capacity.

Learning from how African governments and the private sector have handled technical and vocational education and training programs, for example, it is clear they are not the right institutions to house the above mentioned type of initiative. Mohamoud (2007: 117 – 119) identify the following as some of the weaknesses of government and the private sector in Africa handling technical and vocational education and training programs·

- Government and the private sector did not always come to fully realize that any investment in technical and vocational education is a productive investment, not a cost with significant private and social returns, including the well being of workers, enhanced productivity and international competitiveness.

- Given the immense ongoing or envisaged scientific, technological and socio-economic development that characterizes the new era, particularly globalization and the revolution in information and communication technology, technical and vocational education was not regarded by governments and the private sector as a vital aspect of the educational process in all African countries.

- As economic, social and technological change gathered pace, African decision and policy makers did not realize the great importance of knowledge, competencies and skills to the economic development of the continent and that this development could not be effective without technical and vocational training.

- Technical and vocational education and training programs have long been on the back burner of many African governments' educational policies and development plans. They have always been undervalued, underfinanced and underrated.

- There was no recognition of the economic value of technical and vocational education and training and the vital contribution it could make in raising labor productivity, thus accelerating economic growth and consequently propelling Africa's global economic development at a higher level.

Against this background, the only people who may be interested, who may have the energy and space are university students and other young local entrepreneurs. This group of people would have the advantage of avoiding the usual bureaucracy of established institutions and can connect directly with local contexts and with the communities. This same observation was made by Buckminister Fuller in the 1960s when he championed the need for an 'innovation revolution' led by university students to wipe out world poverty (Fuller, 1969). I am not sure how and where that initiative ended.

The special effort of world science led by university students and the organization proposed above must commit specifically to addressing the unmet challenges of the poor and the high goal of leading Africa to economic independence. Donors, if they are serious in their claim of the development of the continent, have an obligation to support this initiative.

Since the conventional institutions may not be in a hurry to see an economically independent Africa, this is why the above mentioned organization or organizations cannot be organized in the same conventional way civil society organizations are organized. To bring about enough national and continental momentum the organization has to come in the form and force of a social movement maybe more correctly in the force of an economic independence movement with the key success factors mentioned in the chapter on civil society organizations' role in economic independence. These once again being: a deeply resonating, appealing and relevant purpose: economic independence for the continent.

The organization needs legitimate leadership able to connect at a deep, emotional and values level with the students, other entrepreneurs, communities, donors and the other stakeholders. It needs to give space to the students both in forming it and in its running. The organization needs to transcend 'NGOization'. The organization needs to be exemplary in leveraging technology as a means to build up momentum and involvement in the economic independence struggle for the continent.

Most importantly the organization must be results oriented. It must give itself a deadline by which through its efforts, the continent will reach (from pre-agreed indicators) a tipping point for economic independence. If it fails to reach the agreed target and goals by the agreed date, the organization must be humble enough to close down because the failure simply means that this suggested solution is a wrong one. It must close down to give the continent a chance to think of other possible solutions. There are many organizations on the continent that have failed but they still continue to exist. Their leaders are not humble enough to accept the fact that their organizations have failed and therefore lost their relevance. Instead of being part of the solution, they have become part of the very problems they set out to solve. It is rare indeed to see on the continent leaders who step down because they have failed (I only know of the transition president of Somalia who voluntarily stepped down in December 2008 because, he said, he had failed to bring about the change he had hoped to bring). Because leaders do not step down when they fail, their organizations also mirror them as organizations are elongations of the people leading them. They do not close down when it is clear they have failed. It is only businesses which close as there will be no profit to sustain them when they fail to generate the profit. This is a major explanation of the largely ineffective state and civil society institutions on the continent.

Cultivating a business culture

Africans relative to other groups are not traders by conditioning and history. Successful African business people are an exception rather than the norm.

Recently, students of a third year economics class at Kampala University in Uganda were asked whether they would want to start their own businesses after graduating or if they would prefer to be employed by some NGOs or government or some company. Out of a hundred students only three said they would prefer to go into entrepreneurship and business. The rest said they preferred formal employment. The colonial educational system was designed to train Africans to become house servants and gardeners. Those who went further with their education became clerks and professional civil servants. There was no training in entrepreneurship. Businesses and trade were left for Asians and other groups. Unfortunately, this has continued because most post-colonial curricula on the continent have not corrected this anomaly. There is a most urgent need in making formal education more relevant on the continent as *what one wants to see in a country they must first put in schools.*

In addition the very few Africans trying to get into serious business will meet the obstacles of: barriers to entry, lack of finance and the leg up competition of other groups after having kept the Africans out of the game for five hundred years. (I saw the other day consultancy advert in a local African newspaper and the advert clearly said to qualify for the consultancy the applying firm must be Japanese). This is why agriculture collapsed in Zimbabwe after land was given to local Zimbabweans after being confiscated from the white farmers, for example. With the foregoing factors success in business becomes very difficult for most Africans. There is therefore need for deliberate positive discrimination in policies to help Africans catch up. South Korea dealt with this problem by offering tax breaks, soft loans and offering government contracts to local companies.

In the place where I live I observe a group of people who stay 70 km away from the city. These people's business is selling charcoal to the city dwellers (most of whom cannot afford to pay electricity bills for cooking and heating and use the charcoal instead). In order to reach town by 7 am they start off by bicycles at around 2 am each morning. They carry two bags of charcoal of about 15 kg each to sell at a total of $10 each. They have to cycle back the 70 km so that they can start off again the next 2 am. This is how they make their livelihood. Probably their fathers were doing the same and this is the only way they have learnt to make a living. Their sons are also learning from them and will probably end up like them. *The juice is obviously not worth the squeeze* unfortunately, this is the general concept of the meaning of 'business' in much of Africa. Business is not a status occupation. Prospective parents-in-law get very worried when their sons and daughters tell them that their suitors or fiancés are a business person. Business people are in fact and many times perceived to be inferior to civil servants and civil society employees. Unless the concept of business is lifted to the place of significance it has reached in developed countries, we may as well forget about any hope of any economic independence. We cannot develop countries and a continent on mere games of petty businesses of selling two bags of charcoal, a few sugar canes on the road side, a few boiled eggs, some roast ground nuts in a plate measured out with a teaspoon and a few doughnuts, for example, while leaving serious business to other groups of people mostly non-Africans who make real money and send the profits back to their home countries.

The foregoing also emphasizes the need for science and technology to help the poor people come up with more profitable and also environmentally sustainable businesses. When impoverished households are more productive on their farms, they face less pressure to cut down neighboring forests in search for new farmland or to make charcoal to supplement their incomes in very unprofitable and unproductive ways as illustrated above.

Africans need to begin possessing assets and businesses. Because most Africans do not own buildings in which to do business as these belong to other groups of people for example, I observe many times and in many places how these groups will frustrate Africans renting their buildings when they begin making progress. They will just raise the rent to a level that the tenant cannot afford. When they go away, they are quickly replaced with their own people. There is need to own property and positively discriminate for locals who are taking initiative towards the economic independence of their countries and the continent. Foreign businesses can help but they cannot develop a country. For every asset and business owned by other groups on the continent Africans must strive to create African owned parallels.

In creating local parallels, the South Koreans began in the fifties with light manufacture (mainly textiles, especially spinning and weaving) but switched in the 1960s to synthetic fibers and then to chemicals and heavy industries (Mehrotra and Jolly, 1998: 271). Like *the journey of a thousand miles, they started with the first step*. This will require Africans to learn to work together and pool resources for economies of scale and synergy. It is a catching up game and there is a long way to go and it will not help to continue being selfish by insisting on working in isolation. There is need to work together. There is also need to banish national boundary mentality especially for those who have something to offer. It is important to banish national boundary mentality and concentrate on the continent. There is need to form partnerships within and across the artificial borders. There should be no visas on the continent for Africans. Why should Africans pay visas to go to another African country when outsiders who go to the same countries do not?

Currently there is no African technological, economic, political or social brand on the global market. In a globalized world the ultimate goal of owning businesses must be to participate not only locally and internationally but also globally. Any serious reflection on the future of the world economy and therefore the living standards of the billions who inhabit the world will show that a strategic shift towards a significantly larger world economy can only be achieved as a result of raising living standards in the developing countries which would therefore result in the radical expansion of the world markets for capital, goods and services (Mbeki 2001: 186). This is the challenge Africans need to rise up to and the opportunity they need to seize through establishing serious businesses.

Patronizing own businesses

Asians have developed by patronizing their own businesses. Africans will do well to follow their example. *Buy African* must be every African's motto. We must have a new respect for the proper use of our money by watching carefully where it goes and whether that helps to economically empower our communities or not. Those Africans owning businesses on the other hand must be easy to do business with. They should not frustrate fellow Africans by charging exorbitant prices and offering poor quality and poor service. This will only strengthen the economic hold other groups already have on the Africans.

The essence of the above strategy is well summarized by Lee Kuan Yew (2000: 689) when he says – the story of Singapore's progress is a reflection of the advances of the industrial countries – 'their inventions, technology, enterprise and drive. It is part of the story of man's search for new fields to increase his wealth and well being... with each technological advance, Singapore advanced – containers, air travel, air flight, satellite communication, inter-continental fiber optic cables. The technological revolution will bring enormous changes in the next 50 years. Information technology, computers and communications and their manifold uses, the revolution in microbiology, gene therapy, and cloning and organ reproduction will transform people's lives. Singaporeans will have to be nimble in adopting and adapting these new discoveries to play a role in disseminating their benefits' – this is the essence of the five step strategy presented above. In it is the secret of economic independence. This is the route to utopia. This is the hope for Africa. To paraphrase President Ronald Reagan (1999: 855),

> It is time for us to realize that we are too great a nation (continent) to limit ourselves to small dreams. We are not as some would want us believe in a fate that will befall us no matter what we do. I do believe in a fate that will befall us if we do nothing. So with all the creative energy at our command, let us begin an era of continental renewal.

The strategy presented above provides the way to begin realizing this continental renewal and struggle for economic independence. Oblivion and utopia are not predestined. They are a matter of choice.

Conclusion

Africa is at a crossroads. It is faced with oblivion or utopia as real possibilities. Fifty years of aid based development have failed. Close to $ 2.3 trillion of aid has left many people worse off (van Gelder, 2008: 33). Continuing on this path is moving towards oblivion. With increasing desertification from the North of the continent, increased droughts from the South and too much rains in the center in the next ten years (Wiggins and Levy, 2008), and the impact of HIV and AIDS Africa may well be headed for oblivion.

If Africa does not rise up to the challenge of globalization, it will be squeezed out of meaningful existence. Unfortunately, this is already happening as Africa is being talked about less and less in global issues except as a burden with increasing need of aid and as a source of raw materials.

With the natural resource endowment the continent has, investing in *intellect's know-how* to transform the resources to wealth, promises to be the route to utopia as proved over and over again in other countries and regions that have taken this route. South Korea and the top performers on the continent like Botswana have taken this route. The five steps given above provide a rudimentary road map to utopia.

The real damage that history inflicted on Africa through slavery, colonialism and business policies of the dictatorship that took over from the colonialists was suffocating the entrepreneurial spirit on the continent. It was suffocating the invention, innovation and entrepreneurial capacity of the continent. This realization is important because *a problem properly described is a problem half solved*. The realization points out to the solution to the African economic development problem. It suggests that to realize economic development Africa must shift focus from aid dependence (with no end in sight) to dependence on invention, innovation and entrepreneurship for own wealth creation.

Much of what is called bad or corrupt leadership in Africa today is just a reflection of *'scarcity mentality'* among the so-called leaders. Marcus Aurelius said *poverty is the mother of all crimes*. Science through inventions, innovation and entrepreneurship promises abundance for all. If this route is followed, apart from sheer greed common everywhere, much of the leadership and corruption challenges on the continent would disappear. I have an opinion that if some of the best presidents of Europe and America were taken to become president of some African country, they would flounder. They would flounder because for leaders to be effective they need to have the resources they need and a relatively independent economy. This is why we see most of the times especially among NGOs that were prosperous when run by expatriates go down the drain when the expatriate leaves and local leadership takes over. One of the major reasons is that often the departure of the expatriates also mean the departure of financial support in the name of the need for the organization to become 'financially sustainable'. The African problem includes but is much deeper than just incompetent leadership. A situation that allows bad leaders to emerge and people being left powerless to remove such leaders from power is more to blame than the bad leaders themselves who in true sense are not leaders.

The future of Africa is in organizing for and refocusing to invention, innovation and entrepreneurship and not in aid. The current aid-led strategy has taken us where we are today and all indicators are that continuing with this strategy will only lead to oblivion. It is time to stop the current beehive of aid activity and change course. As the proverb says, *what is the point of running so fast when you are on the wrong road?*

The above laid five-point strategy could be the road to utopia. Paul Tillich said *we cannot be born anew if the power of the old is not broken within us*. We need to break the entrenched power of non-developmental donor dependence so that we can give birth to our economic independence. Fortunately, we are at a time when there is some soul searching among some donor agencies on where they could have missed it and how they can move forward. This book suggests that if such 'soul searching initiatives' are truly genuine the way forward would be to make sure that aid contributes significantly enough towards building entrepreneurial and business power and balancing this with ensuring effective states and a vibrant civil society

We have learnt the lesson that asking the question *'How can Africa become economically independent'* should in fact be directed at ourselves. We have learnt that it is not wise to be asking other people questions that we should be asking ourselves. We have also learnt that it is not always right to listen just to anybody simply because they are speaking. Not many people know what they are talking about. The economic situation we are in today attests to this. The so many voices we have listened to in the past have led us where we are today.

As Henry David Thoreau once said, "A good book teaches better than to read it. I must soon lay it down and commence living by its hint. What I began by reading I must finish by acting". If each one of us can lay down this book and begin living by the hint of the five step strategy, the book will have accomplished its mission.

I would like to end by quoting Chinua Achebe from his book, the *Trouble with Nigeria*: "We have lost the twentieth century; are we bent on seeing that our children also lose the twenty-first? God forbid"!

BIBLIOGRAPHY

Achebe, C. *The Trouble with Nigeria*. Londond: Heinemann, 1983.

Amoako, K. "Ghana's Economic Transition." Paper Presented at the Launch of Economic History of Ghana: Reflections of Half a Century of Challenges and Progress, Accra, Ghana, October 30, 2008.

Bawnegie, D. 2008. "Asia's Economic Transformation: India's Role in an Emerging International Order." *IPCS Issue Brief* no 70 (June 2008).

Calderisi, R. *The Trouble with Africa: Why Foreign Aid isn't Working*. London: Yale University Press, 2007.

Canfield, J. *How to Get from Where You Are to Where You Want to Be: The 25 Principles of Success*. London: Harper Collins Publishers Ltd, 2007.

Castro, F. *My Life*. London: Penguin Books, 2007.

Chikago, J. *Crossing Cultural Frontiers*. Blnatyre: Montfort Press, 2003.

Clavell, J. *The Art of War*. London: Hodder and Stoughton Ltd, 1981.

Commonwealth Foundation. *Framework for Action on Maximizing Civil Society's Contribution to Development and Democracy*. London: Commonwealth Foundation, 2004.

Diamond, J. *Collapse: How Societies Choose to Fail or Survive*. London: Allen Lane, 2005.

Dorman, S. "Rocking the Boat? Church NGOs and Democratization in Zimbabwe." *African Affairs* 101, no. 402 (2002) 75-92.

Edwards, M and Fowler, A. *The Earthscan Reader on NGO Management*. London: Earthscan, 2002.

Edwards, M. "Have NGOs 'Made a Difference?' From Manchester to Birmingham with an Elephant in the Room." GPRG Conference, University of Manchester. Manchester. 27-29 June 2005, 2005.

Escobar, A. "The Making and Unmaking of the Third World through Development." *The Post Development Reader*. London: Zed Books, 1997.

Fowler, A. "Civil Society Research Findings from a Global Perspective: A Case for Redressing Bias, Asymmetry and Bifurcation." *Voluntas* 13, no. 3 (2002): 287-300.

Fowler, A. "Aid Architecture: Reflections on NGDO Futures and the Emergence of Counter-Terrorism." *INTRAC Occasional Paper Series* no 45, 2005.

Fuller, Buckminister, R. *Utopia or Oblivion: the Prospects for Humanity*. London: Bantam Books, 1969.

Goussikindy, E. *The Impact of Culture on African Political and Economic Development: A Riddle for Policy Makers*. Georgetown: Woodstock-Berkley, 2006.

Govindarajan, V and Gupta, A. *The Quest for Global Dominance: Transforming Global Presence into Global Competitive Advantage*. San Francsisco: Jossey-Bass, 2001.

Greenleaf, R. *Servant Leadership: A Journey through the Nature of Legitimate Power and Greatness*. Paulist Press International, 2001.

Gupta, s et al. "Making Remittances Work for Africa." *Finance and Development* 44, no. 22 (2007).

Haley, A. *The Autography of Malcom X*. New York: Ballantine Books, 1965.

Hancock, G. *The Lords of Poverty*. London: Camerapix Publishers International, 2004.

Handy, C. *Myself and other More Important Matters*. London: Arrow Books, 2006.

Harden, B. *Africa: Dispatches from a Fragile Continent*. London: Harper Collins Publishers, 1993.

Hill, N. *Think and Grow Rich*. London: Vermilion, 2004.

Kaldor, M. "Civil Society and Accountability." *Journal of Human Development* 4, no 1 (2003): 5-26.

Kamara, S and Yeboah, H. "Bringing the Poor into Advocacy: A Look at Ghana HIPC Watch." *PLA Note* 51, (2005): 32-38.

Kaplan, A. *The Development Practitioner's Handbook*. London: Pluto Press, 1996.

Korten, D. *When Corporations Rule the World*. London: Earthscan, 1995.

Kyaruzi, I. *African Business and Economic Growth: Institutions, Firms, Practices and Policy*, London: Adonis & Abbey Publishers.

Kynge, J. *China Shakes the World: The Rise of a Hungry Nation*. London: Phoenix, 2006.

Lamb, D. *The Africans*. New York: Vintage Books, 1987.

Landes, D. *The Wealth and Poverty of Nations*. London: Little and Brown Company, 2001.

Legwaila, L. "Natural Resources and Conflict in Africa: Transforming a Peace Liability to a Peace Asset." Conference Proceedings, Egypt, Cairo, 17-19 June, 2006.

Livegoed, B. *The Developing Organization*. London: Tavistock, 1973.

Livegoed, B. *Managing the Developing Organization*. London: Oxford, 1969.

Lonnqvist, L. "China's Aid to Africa: Implications for Civil Society." Policy Briefing Paper 17, *INTRAC*, 2008.

Maathai, W. "Bottle-Necks of Development in Africa." 4th UN World Conference. United Nations. Beijing, China. August 30-September 15, 1995.

Mansfield, S. *Derek Prince: A Biography*. Florida: Charisma House, 2005.

Masset, E and White, H. "Are Chronically Poor People being Left Out of Progress towards the Millennium Development Goals? A Quantitative Analysis of Older People, Disabled People and Orphans." *Journal of International Human Development* 5, no. 2 (2004): 279-297.

Mbeki, T. Mahube: *The Dawning of the Dawn*. Braamfontein: Skotaville Media, 2001.

Mehrotra, S and Jolly, R. *Development with a Human Face: Experiences in Social Achievement and Economic Growth*. Oxford: Clarendo Press, 1998.

Meredith, M. *The State of Africa: the History of Fifty Years of Independence*, Cape Town: Jonathan Ball Publishers, 2006.

Mohamoud, A, ed. *Shaping a New Africa*. Amsterdam: KIT Publishers, 2007.

Nkwachukwu, O. "'Conventional' Notion of Civil Society, International Civil Society Organizations and the Development of Civil Society in Africa." International Civil Society Forum. Ulaanbaar, Mongolia. 8-9 September, 2003.

Norman, E. *Christianity and the World Order*. Oxford: Oxford University Press, 1979.

Ohmae, K. *The Mind of the Strategist: The Art of Japanese Business*. New York: McGraw-Hill, Inc, 1982.

Onyeani, C. *Capitalist Nigger: The Road to Success*. Johannesburg: Joanathan Ball Publishers, 2000.

Patel, K. *The Master Strategist: Power, Purpose and Principle*. London: Arrow Books, 2005.

Poole, N. "Promoting Efficient Markets." *Footsteps 77*, December, 2008.

Rahnema, M. and Bawtree, V. *The Post-Development Reader*. London: Zed Books, 1997.

Reagan, R. First Inaugural Address, January 20, 1981. *World's Greatest Speeches* edited by Lewis Copeland, Lawrence Lamm and Stephen McKenna. New York: Dover Publications, 1999.

Rogers, E. *The Diffusion of Innovation*. New York: The Free Press, 1983.

Rothwell, J and Sullivan, R. *Practicing Organization Development*. San Francisco: Pfeiffer, 2005.

Sachs, I. *Gandhi and Development: A European View in Self Reliance: A Strategy for Development*. London: Bogle-L'Ouverture Publications Ltd, 1980.

Sachs, J. *The End of Poverty: How We Can Make It Happen In Our Lifetime*. London: Penguin, 2005.

Schwab, P. *Africa: A Continent Self-Destructs*. New York: Palgrave, 2001.

Shapiro, R. *Future Cast: A Global Vision of Tomorrow*. London: Profile Books, 2008.

Stewart, T. *Intellectual Capital: The New Wealth of Organizations*. New York: Doubleday, 1997.

Thekaekara, M. "Direct Trade that Benefits the Poor in India and the UK." *LEISA* 24, no. 1 (2008)

United Nations, *Resource Flows to Africa: An Update on Statistical Trends*. New York: UN, 2005.

Van Gelder, A. "Unleashing Africa's Growth." The *Daily Times*, Friday, 19 Sept. 2008: 33

Washington, J. *A Testament of Hope: The Essential Writings and Speeches of Martin Luther King Jr*. New York: Harper Collins Publishers, 1991.

Wiggins, S and Levy, S. "Rising Food Prices: Cause for Concern." *Natural Resources Perspectives* 115, (2008): 1-4.

World Bank, *Engaging Civil Society Organizations in Conflict Affected and Fragile States, Three African Country Case Studies*, Report no. 32538-GLB, 2005.

Yew, Kuan Lee, *From Third World to First World: The Singapore Story (1965-2000)*. New York: Harper Collins Publishers, 2000.

APPENDIX: A SUMMARY OF THE DISCUSSION ON THE FUTURE OF AFRICA

Introduction

A group of Africans from different countries met at Hotel Panorama in Antananarivo in Madagascar on the night of 26th August, 2008 to discuss the plight of the African continent. The discussion centered on trying to understand what the priority African challenge today is and how this challenge can be articulated in a way that can enable intelligent debate on the way forward for the continent. This paper summarizes the deliberations by discussing the immediate past of the continent and how this has shaped the present. It then discusses the key priority issues Africa is facing today and their implications for the immediate and long term future. The author concludes the paper by showing that Africa is caught up in a situation where it is forced to 'grow before it is ready' or where it is forced to jump some stages of development which is naturally a very difficult thing to happen.

The essence of the paper is that Africa's solution lies in own wealth creation through innovations and inventions as an alternative to the present capitalist system that by its nature does not create wealth but redistributes already existing wealth by concentrating it in the hands of the few at the top and away from the poor people at the bottom. The paper also attempts to show that much of the current aid system is part of the capitalist system and therefore not developmental in nature.

The past

The first leaders on the continent were committed to people's well being. They were ideologically rooted and there were high levels of intellectualism. Examples of ideologies included Julius Nyerere's *Ujamaa*, Kenneth Kaunda's *Humanism* and Jomo Kenyatta's *Harambee*. This, however, was interrupted by the cold war (between capitalist and communism ideologies especially between USA and the Soviet Union). Both sides condoned leaders even corrupt ones as long as they showed their support to their side. This also pitted leaders on the continent against each other escalating levels of civil and national wars on the continent. This was the beginning of the derailing of Africa's development after the end of colonialism.

While Africa was making economic progress and even better progress than many countries in South Asia, a reversal happened around the 1980s when the continent actually began to move backwards. Around this time, Africa lost its share of the world market to other developing regions that had become more productive and efficient. Africa was losing $70 million per year and turned to the World Bank and IMF who proposed structural adjustments as the solution to help out. The solution, however, proved to be a 'medicine that was too strong for the disease'. In short, structural adjustments left much of Africa even poorer. It should be emphasized that the root problem was not the structural adjustment programs but the loss of productivity of the African economies. Logically the solution would be to improve the productivity of the economies to a level that would catch up and compete fairly with the other economies. This is what structural adjustment programs failed to achieve.

The fall of the Berlin wall in 1989 signified the fall of communism which meant, the USA was left as a single super power in the world. This was followed by the push for US style of democracy around the world. Countries like South Africa took advantage of this wind of opportunity and swiftly brought an end to apartheid. Many countries on the continent also introduced multiparty democracies.

A key lesson in the introduction of democracy was that democracy works well where the 3 centers of power are well established. These are the state, the economy and the civil society. This means opportunities for exercising power are distributed among the three centers reducing unhealthy competition for power. The strength of the 3 centers of power explains why South Africa was able to take advantage of the democracy opportunity. In much of Africa, however, the economy and the civil society were not as well developed leaving only the state as the sole center of power. In South Africa, for example, a possible conflict or struggle for power between Thabo Mbeki and Cyril Ramaphosa was averted because Ramaphosa went to the economy (business) and Mbeki went to the state. In many African countries there is no life outside the state function because one cannot exercise power through business or the civil society as these are not well developed. This is creating intense competition for people to get into government through politics (elections). Those in power do not want to go out while those who are not in power would like to displace those who are in power. In America, for example, when a party loses an election, the people go back to their normal lives maybe in universities, businesses or other means of livelihood. In Africa you go back to poverty or to jail.

The 3 centers of power are supposed to be partners in development and they are supposed to work at strengthening each other. Unfortunately, in many countries in Africa governments look at civil society as enemies and work against them. Examples include introduction of bills aimed at crippling the voice of the civil society. Unfortunately, when there is a choice to be made between government and civil society many donors choose to stand with governments even if it means going against the very values they claim to stand for.

The present
The fall of communism ushered in the age of unchecked capitalism. Capitalism thrives on the accumulation of wealth from the masses to a few at the top. Capitalism as it is practiced and observed in Africa, does not produce wealth but transfers wealth from the poor at the bottom to the rich at the top. This has led to an acute increase in poverty among the masses. The key challenge is how to redistribute capital. States have become sources of making money for politicians in power. They collude with businesses to exploit the poor. There are no effective checks and balances as the civil society is generally weak. Politicians are the ones controlling local businesses. In some countries presidents and their close friends control up to 50% of the economy in private

businesses. In addition, they also collude with multinationals to do extractive businesses at the expense of the well being of the people. Capitalism has increased rather than decreased poverty on the continent.

Civil society organizations in the North have failed to play a 'watch dog role' on how the capitalist policies of their governments are creating poverty in the South. Before Africa got defeated, the civil society in the North failed. An example is where governments in the North permits their companies to come and do exploitative businesses in Africa (like getting oil or mineral resources at very cheap prices), creating poverty in the process. They then get taxes from the same companies and give them to their NGOs to fight the very poverty that their companies created in the first place. The problem is the money that comes back in the form of aid is just a minute fraction of the money that is extracted by the companies, for example.

Wealth creation and redistribution of wealth needs a healthy balance among the state, the economy (business) and the civil society – with the civil society holding the two in check. The trajectory of humanity has reached a stage where capital is the key dominant feature. They key challenge now is to move from this competitive stage to the cooperative and interdependent stage. A healthy balance of the 3 centers of power is critical if this shift is to be realized.

In addition to the rise of capitalism, we have the challenge of climate change. Climate change is going to hit Africa the hardest. There are predictions of increased desertification from the North of the continent, increased droughts from the Southern part of the continent and too much rain along the equator in the center of the continent. Currently, the three countries that can potentially feed the whole continent (DRC, Zimbabwe and Sudan) are in conflict. This scenario is likely to create a perfect storm on the continent in the next few years.

Bare knuckle and cut throat globalization is shrinking resources available even in Europe. This is leading to policies that will result in less and less aid money coming to Africa as these countries have to take care of their own home problems first. The decentralization policies of Northern NGOs (seeking presence in the South) are an expression of realizing that they do not have enough power by themselves.

The above discussion presents a very complex situation that makes solutions seem impossible. In the words of one participant in the discussion,

> What should be our African response? I am confused. The issues are so complicated. I do not know how to respond or to interpret what is happening because I am part of the problem. I benefit from the system that is creating poverty to my people. I may be secure but what about my children and their future? My country is so poor; no one is listening any more… when I go home from here I will find people queuing on my door begging for money. People are so poor, it is very depressing, I just wish I went back to the 1970s when life was so good.

Can we provide an alternative that can give people real hope – to move them from the deepest to the highest they can reach? The key challenge is what type of leadership is required to interpret these phenomena and strategize for rapid and adequate spreading of wealth? What political configuration can best organize in the interest of the poor given that capitalism organizes around trade which the poor do not have access to and that the capitalist system is geared towards serving a few people, not all?

If businesses and the state have colluded and they do not have the interests of the poor at heart, the only hope is in a selfless civil society that would effectively 'force' the state and the business to serve the interests of the poor people through effective social and economic accountability efforts. The strength of the civil society defines the people centeredness of the state and the businesses in the country. This is supposed to be the normal setting. This is what happened in Europe soon after the second world war when civil society organizations sprang up to start forcing their governments to take the interests of the people to heart and to extend this to the developing regions of the world as well. All the big NGOs in post war Europe were also an expression of balancing the power of capitalism with the interests of the poor. Today, however, this balancing of power in Europe is not as strong it was then. Today civil society is retreating while as at the same time capitalism is advancing.

The future

The state matters because it is the only mechanism mandated to take care of the citizens in providing basic needs that businesses or civil society cannot provide. Currently, the living conditions of the people on the continent are getting worse because states have abdicated their responsibilities as the civil society is too weak to *hold them effectively accountable.* Part of the solution to the African problem is to strengthen the social and economic accountability role of the civil society organizations.

In addition to building their capacity for social and economic accountability, the civil society need to take on an additional role in contributing towards wealth creation. This is because aid on its own is inadequate to bring about the fundamental economic changes to lift Africa to a level where it can begin to catch up with the other continents. Civil society organizations need to lobby the centers of learning on the continent to come up with break through innovations and inventions that can lift millions of people out of poverty.

In the last 50 years no major scientific breakthroughs have come out of Africa. The way to *create wealth* is compounding (natural) resources through intellect's know-how. The aid system may be designed in such a way that it makes fundamental economic shifts impossible but one does not need a license to invent and innovate and thus create wealth. One, however, does need support to get the inventions and innovations to the market. This is the support that civil society organizations need to provide through lobbying for more investment, organization, promotion and protection of the inventions and innovation.

In practical terms, in terms of *wealth distribution*, to move forward it will be necessary to:

- Recognize the fact that capitalism needs people (the poor people who are many). This is capitalism's weaknesses that provides an opportunity of a solution for the poor people.
- Capitalism cannot do away with people. Money is produced by people and not by money. The poor people are the geese that lay the golden eggs. For example, capitalism needs the poor coffee farmer from Ethiopia. The issue is in the chain to the coffee on the table in Europe. It is in this chain where the problems of lack of fairness to the farmer are and how to deal with those problems is the point of intervention.
- As capital grows, it deepens its dependence on the same people. It is also important to recognize that capitalism is a juggernaut that pushes until the poor people cannot take it anymore. Their lived experience then propels them to a revolution. This is the natural course of events but it needs not happen if the poor people are empowered to recognize their power for negotiation.
- The hope of the poor is in empowering them in their negotiation power in the production process. This is where the role of civil society organizations comes in. If there is a universal or at least continent-wide conscientization of the bargaining power of the poor people, capitalism will have no choice but to bend to the will of the people. This calls for powerful organizations that represent the interests and voices of the poor. Often times the poor people are their own victims – by the way they look at the world and the way they define success. They collude with the system. The ideology of being dominated is isolated hence the need for conscientization.

In terms of *wealth creation*, it will be important to invent an alternative to capitalism. This would mean inventing a system that would create enough for all, making competitive capitalism irrelevant. There is need to invest in wealth creation on the continent. This is an issue that much of the current aid system does not even mention.

Capitalism does not produce capital or wealth in the real sense of the word. It only redistributes the wealth upwards. Wealth is created through high magnitude innovations and inventions that can lift millions of people out of poverty. This is a challenge for the institutions of higher learning and research centers; and calls for novel type of civil society organizations that would organize to take the ideas, innovations and inventions to the market for the benefit of all. The issue is to create an alternative to 'greedy' capitalism by ensuring that there is enough to go round for everyone. When there is enough to go round for everyone, competition and war become obsolete. The ability to do this would signify a key shift from the independent/competitive stage to the interdependent stage of human development.

The state too does not produce wealth. It only distributes. Businesses (at least capitalism) do not produce wealth they only distribute and concentrate wealth upwards into the hands of a few people. Civil society does not produce wealth. It only checks the behavior of the state and the businesses in the interests of the citizens. Only applied science or technology through innovations and inventions produce wealth – as wealth is energy compounded by intellect's know-how. If a person discovers a cure for AIDS, for example, that person will become very rich and his or her country will greatly benefit through taxes. If he or she is a philanthropist a lot of people will also benefit directly. This is how wealth is created. The continent therefore must organize innovation and inventions into a fourth power (in addition to the state, civil society, the economy) and entrust it with the responsibility to create wealth.

There are numerous brilliant innovations and inventions from most universities on the continent but these never go beyond the lab as there is no mechanism to bring them to the market. Civil society, because they exist for the common good, should get the additional role to promote the innovations from idea to the market and protecting the innovations and the inventions from being hijacked. The innovations and inventions do not have to be original. They may as well just be adaptations of the ones that already exist. In addition civil society should take an additional role to monitor and advocate for a curriculum that would promote creativity and self reliance and a strong foundation for innovation and inventions. In the words of a Reverend, William Murray, *What you want to see in a country, first put it in schools.* There is need to promote and organize the institutions of higher learning and research centers and other innovators and inventors into the fourth center of power (in addition to the state, the civil society and business). We need to grow a pool of educated, intelligent young people armed with the technical know-how of America, Europe and Japan to lead us in the catching up game of transforming our resources into wealth as our friends have done in China, India, Singapore and South Korea.

The wealth thus created would offer an alternative to non-developmental aid. This is not to say that we do not need aid. Aid to be truly developmental must be seen as a transition measure with a clear end in sight. For aid to be truly developmental it must contribute towards wealth creation on the continent and for the continent and not only distribution through the state or civil society organizations. The nature of the aid debate needs to move beyond better quantity and quality aid to include aid supporting the creation of own wealth for the continent.

Conclusion

An interpretation of what is happening today is that the world in general is in a crisis to shift from the independent/competitive stage of development to the interdependent/cooperative stage of development. This shift is affecting the different parts of the world differently and it is also manifesting itself in the different parts of the world differently. Africa is in a more peculiar situation because, it has not had an opportunity to truly develop to its own level of economic independence and therefore economic competitiveness on the globe and yet it is being forced to sublimate to the interdependent stage. This is a very peculiar position because a natural system or entity cannot jump a stage of development. This will require real hard thinking on how to make Africa economically independent in the shortest time possible so that it can catch up with the rest of the world in the struggle towards economic interdependence.

This means that as of today most of the benefits of globalization are beyond the reach of most Africans.

Suggestions offered in this paper are beginning to point towards a contextually relevant model that may get us out of the quagmire. In short, the conclusions are suggesting that the current system of capitalism was developed in response to Malthus' assertion that there isn't enough in the world to go round for everyone. But now it has been proven beyond any shadow of doubt that in fact, it is possible to have enough to go round for present and future needs of 100% of humanity. This, however, has not been realized in Africa and this line of debate has not really been pursued. We have not asked how we can multiply the value of Africa's resources to ensure plenty for all and where we would look for leadership in this pursuit. It is clear that business people and the state left alone would not have this in their interest as it would be seen as something that would weaken their power and relevance. The revolution to have enough for all at the magnitude of the green revolution in Asia, for example, would be led by the civil society and institutions of higher learning through high inventions and innovations that can lift millions of people out of poverty.

The people who control wealth are the ones who control the world. It is naïve to think that those people will share their wealth and therefore power with anyone else. The only way to play the game is create your own wealth. Fortunately the highway to wealth has now been opened and anybody is free to walk in it. The institutions of higher learning, research centers and civil society are possibly where people can begin to look up to for leadership but the question is: Are the civil society organizations and the institutions of higher learning on the continent able to rise up to the challenge?

Index

loans, to jump-start industry, 71;
promoting local, 73–74, 108;
supporting, African owned, 87,
90, 113
Buy African, as motto, 90, 113

Calderisi, R., 103–5
capital, 18; coming from abroad,
91; globalization and, 9; lack of,
17
capitalism, 124–26, 127;
monopolies *vs.*, 46, 90;
redistributing wealth through,
121, 125; wealth transfer from,
122–23
The Capitalist Nigger, 63, 106
Castro, F., 46, 69–70, 90
CDRA. *See* Community
Development Association South
Africa
charismatic churches. *See* churches
China, 18–19, 75, 83, 100; Africa
vs., as sleeping giant, 19;
balancing world power, 47;
economic reforms and, 7; as
major geopolitical force, 78–79;
selling culture, to world, 82;
young people, as optimistic, 101
Chisanu, Joachim, 62
churches, 37, 42
circle of influence, assessing, 36
citizenship program, backfiring, 22
civil society, 6, 41–42, 52, 124;
ending exploitation and, 70;
government working against,
122; holding
government/business
accountable, 20, 98; need for
international, 44–47, 90;
retreating/weak, 124; role of
religion in, 48
Civil Society Organization(s)
(CSO), 6, 34, 38, 124;
composition of, 41–42; economic
development and, 43–44;

empowering citizens and, 48–49;
targeting privileged young adults,
37; transcending NGOization,
52–53
climate change, challenge of, 14,
23, 47, 77, 123
colonialization, 56–57, 63
commodities, unavailability of, 12
communication, writing as, 26–28
communism, fall of, 122
community, African, 93, 98;
culture of, 13–14; economy of,
11–12; ideal, 94–97; politics of,
12–13; shopping center/bank in,
95
Community Development
Association South Africa
(CDRA), 98
competition: avoiding head to-
head, 87; for government jobs,
122; monopolies *vs.*, 90; prices
vs., 46; wealth through trade and,
18
Concerned Citizens, 33, 50–53
consciousness, creating continental,
3–4
consumer, products/imagination, 4
Conte, Lasana, 12
credit crunch, 77
crisis, African vulnerability to, 18
CSO. *See* Civil Society
Organization
culture, iv, 59–60, 61, 82;
borrowing and lending in, 64;
disintegration of African, in
community, 13–14; of
economically liberated Africa,
97; economic development and,
55–56; globalization, and values,
66–67; shift, from oral to
reading, 26–28; standards setting
as part of, 85–86; ubuntu, 56–57,
65, 69, 78, 81–82, 90

debt cancellation, 19, 85

ABOUT THE AUTHOR

Chiku Malunga is an author and a consultant with many years experience of organization development and development practice work among African, European and American non – profits, NGOs and civil society organizations. He holds a doctorate degree in Development Studies from the University of South Africa. He is currently the director of Capacity Development Consultants (CADECO), an organization that promotes African- centered organizational improvement models.

Chiku's interest is in playing a bridging role through contextualizing the language and concepts of organization and institutional development in particular and development practice in general developed in Europe and America for more relevance in the developing regions of the world; and using Africa's indigenous wisdom to enrich the organizational and development theories and practice in the developed regions of the world. Chiku carries out this bridging mission through writing, consultancy and speaking engagements. His other books include: *Understanding Organizational Sustainability through African Proverbs*, *Making Strategic Plans Work: Insights from African Indigenous Wisdom* and *Understanding Organizational Leadership through Ubuntu.*